T0246059

.

GEORGE BROWN

TOO HOT

Kool & the Gang & Me

CHICAGO
REVIEW
PRESS

Published by Chicago Review Press Incorporated
814 North Franklin Street
Chicago, Illinois 60610
ISBN 978-1-64160-918-0

Library of Congress Control Number: 2023932722

Typesetting: Nord Compo

Printed in the United States of America
5 4 3 2 1

CONTENTS

———

ACKNOWLEDGMENTS

FIRST I'D LIKE TO THANK MY CHILDREN: Dorian Brown, Jorge Brown, Gregory Brown, Jordan Brown, and Aaron Brown. Without them, I wouldn't be in so much trouble! And of course thanks to my wife, Hahn Phan-Brown. Thanks also to my brother, Michael Brown, and my sister, Arlene Brown.

Next I'd like to thank Dave and Joel Brokaw, good friend and attorney David Glinert, long-time friend Maria Papapetros, friend and business partner Claude Ismael, Jonathan Azu for having faith in all my projects, and my friend Linda Salvin, without whom the phone call to my agent would never have been made.

Finally, thanks to my publisher, Chicago Review Press, for believing in me and my story. Also thank you to my collaborator Dave Smitherman for putting up with me for many months. Last but not least, thanks to my literary agent, Diane Nine, for making all of this possible.

1

INTRO

I SEE MY STORY AS A CAUTIONARY TALE, a fantastical narrative of fortune and fame, but one that came at a price. It started innocently enough—me as a talented teenager with a dream to create a band with his equally talented friends—and that group went on to reach musical stardom on a global scale.

Though it might have looked perfect from the outside, navigating the inner workings of a musical juggernaut like Kool & the Gang demanded herculean compromise and concessions.

Regardless of the challenges I've faced, I'm grateful for the band and the journey. The music has taught me valuable life lessons on the importance of perseverance, patience, collaboration, creativity, well-being, and relationships.

Jersey City Shuffle

What gave the Jersey neighborhood of my youth such character was how it stood out as a composite of two worlds. While the hustle and grit ebbed and flowed from the busy city, most folks in our tight-knit community had migrated from rural life in the South in search of a better future for their families. Money was scarce, but folks were rich in southern manners and hospitality, placing great importance on family, friends, and above all, God.

While collectively facing a plethora of social issues, our surprisingly close and caring community was strengthened by a shared determination to achieve a better life. It was customary to greet each other with a "What's happening, brother?" or "How are you, sister?" whether we knew each other or not. People were genuinely concerned about one another's welfare and determined to help out where they could, especially when it came to the youth. In return, the kids coming up during that time were expected to treat adults with respect.

The grownups in the neighborhood moved through each day with unspoken unity. If a kid got into a bit of mischief, there was nowhere to hide. Grown folks had no issue with correcting a child's behavior, especially if they knew the parents were at work earning disproportionately low wages as they tried to provide a better future for their family. No one had to remind us how "it takes a village to raise a child." That was standard practice.

On a street east of Lincoln High School, I loved the juxtaposition of the chickens and goats grazing in their pens as the skyscraper landscape framed their background. Near the theater on Monticello Avenue, the smells of fried fish and smoked barbecued chicken, beef, and pork wafted through the air.

The row houses in the alley behind Ingwersen Place were numbered one through eight on one side of the street, with a fence running just opposite. There were garbage cans beside every door. When I was old enough, I had the job of taking those cans to the end of the alley for our neighbors. I stacked them one on top of another and returned them to their respective places after the Tuesday collection.

We lived in one of those row houses, next door to my cousins, and there was an abandoned lumberyard just behind it. Snapping turtles that had been fished out of the lakes at Lincoln Park were strung up on a line above an overgrown field of untamed Bermuda grass, discarded furniture, and rusted-out refrigerators. Once completely drained of blood, the turtles were de-shelled and cooked at neighborhood barbecues.

In our home, basic comforts like heat and hot water were never guaranteed. To keep the pipes from freezing in the winter, we had to leave the cold water taps open and trickling: *drip, drip, drip* all night long. In the living room that doubled as a bedroom for my parents and sister, there was the menacing stove where the occasional burning ember would escape and sear an everlasting mark in the battered wood floor. It was the kind of stove we'd see in western movies, some cowboy striking a match on the sole of his boot to get the fire started. My brother and I shared a tiny room that was no larger than a walk-in closet. The walls of our house were sparse, and the only picture that always remained was that of Jesus watching over our little family.

Telephone communication consisted of a single "party line" that was shared among all the houses on the block. We followed the honor system: If someone was using the phone line, we hung up immediately so as not to listen in on their conversation. If there was an emergency, we were allowed to politely ask if they could hang up so we could call for help.

One of the things I loved about our home was that music was always playing, and from the beginning I was totally and completely entranced. When the music came on, it probably looked like I was daydreaming, my mind enveloped in a separate reality of tones, beats, and melodies. I loved how my father would come home and walk up the steps to the bathroom singing the undulating jazz phrasing of "Moody's Mood for Love," because that meant he was in a good mood. It amazed me that such a tortured soul could possess such a wonderful, emotive singing voice.

My mother's phonograph was in constant rotation as it filled the house with the sounds of Tito Puente, Eddie Palmieri, Tito Rodríguez, and others. Her love for that style of music was probably a by-product of her Spanish-Portuguese bloodline mixed in with German, African, and Native American. Like my father she had a lovely voice and was an aspiring singer in her late teens. Patrons of the small New York City clubs where she performed often compared her to Sarah Vaughan.

Since those early days, I have never been a great sleeper. During those nights in the twin bed in that tiny room that I shared with my brother, my thoughts were always filled with music. It would sometimes start with the murmur of a childlike soprano voice inside my head, just one note and a solitary voice, then *bam!* I could hear an entire symphony orchestra, each instrument joining in on the fun until they were all represented in melodic unity. In the beginning, it kept me awake all night. But eventually I learned to control it by guiding the symphony to its natural conclusion. It was like a game inside my head, and I was the conductor directing each instrument, making the music bend and shift at will. I'd have the violins play a line, the woodwinds another, and soon an entire composition filled my brain with nocturnal bliss until it finally subsided, allowing me to grab a few precious hours of sleep.

Intuitively I realized that my nocturnal concerts were not something I should discuss but should keep secret, my own private experience. I didn't read a lot into it. I just learned to love the episodes, to give in to them. It was no different than how my friends covertly read comic books under a blanket with a flashlight. But on a subtler level, it was a gift of an unexpected kind. Somehow its presence conveyed to me a deep confidence that I was going to be OK despite the turmoil that surrounded me—especially with my father.

When my dad was seventeen, he was based in San Diego, where he served in the Navy during World War II. During that time, being in military service as a person of color was challenging. Black men were relegated to tasks focused on catering to the others, such as cleaning, cooking, and doing the laundry. However, because Dad had a muscular build, he made something of a name for himself as a ship-to-ship boxer. His success in the ring provided him a modicum of clout, particularly for a Black man. That lasted until a back injury brought his boxing career to an abrupt end, and with it any social sway he might have previously enjoyed.

Once discharged from the Navy, he planned to move back to Jersey and become a police officer. That was probably a natural transition for many service members who had become accustomed to the rigidity and precision of military life. Dad was able to pass the written test, but that back injury prevented him from meeting the physical requirements.

Eventually he was hired by the George Fangman Company, where he worked as a coal man for fourteen years. His duties included shoveling, bagging, and carrying 150-pound bags of coal on his back and then sending them down a chute to an awaiting truck bed. Then he'd deliver the shipments in an eighteen-wheeler with his White driving partner and start all over again. Most days they both wore old bandanas tied over their mouth and nose in hopes of minimizing the amount of coal dust they inhaled. The two men were quite a sight, because the coal dust gave them practically the same ashen complexion. Such physical labor helped to build my dad's rock-hard muscles while weakening his lungs and already compromised spine.

Sometimes, my dad found extra work making truck deliveries. If he went to the nearby mental institution, the staff often gave him some meats and cheeses to bring home, and we were always excited by the unexpected treats. He worked hard to provide for our family while maintaining his pride, but it was clear that the economic deck was stacked against not only him but everyone in our community. Some dealt with the challenges better than others. My father turned to alcohol to cope with his lot in life, and that led to a myriad of psychological problems as well. When he got drunk, he unleashed his fury on anyone in his path. There were frequent clashes with law enforcement, and once, they even secured him in straps that he snapped off like they were made of paper. He would say to them, "I'll bounce you like a rubber ball" or "I'll smash you flatter than a pancake."

On the flip side, he could be fun and lighthearted if he was in a good mood. When I was around six or seven, he used to let me hang around with him. "Don't worry," he'd tell Mom, "I'll mind Georgie. He will be just fine." We'd end up at the local bar listening to his favorite music while I drank ginger ale through a straw, my legs dangling off a battered wooden stool.

Those were some of my favorite times because it was just him and me, and he was in his element, surrounded by good music and strong drinks, the pressures of life a million miles away. He seemed to know the words to every song that came on the jukebox, especially the soulful standards of James Moody, Sarah Vaughan, and Ella Fitzgerald. As he sang along in his baritone voice, it was clear that he had an innate appreciation for not only the vocals but also the musicianship. He kept time with the beat of the song by thumping imaginary sticks on the bar top and then switched effortlessly to strumming a guitar or plucking a bass.

When I saw my father in such a good mood, I wanted it to last forever. As afternoon inched its way toward night, I knew we would have to leave soon, and life would revert back to normal.

On Sundays, if he wasn't hungover, my father made what he called hoe cake. It was like a poor man's bread with flour, milk, and shortening. Then he'd pull out the big, deep iron skillet from the drawer under the stove and place it on the burner as my brother, my sister, and I sat at the table watching him work. He'd mix in eggs and maybe some bacon. Then he'd cook up some grits to go with it.

The three of us would laugh as we watched him sing songs and prepare food for the family. Those were the rare times when the three of us had our father all to ourselves. There was no one to pull his attention away, no distractions, no alcohol to muddy his mind. It was a side of his personality I wish more people had seen, but I was grateful for those Sundays, even if they became increasingly rare as we got older, and the destructive cycle of behavior more frequent.

Dad would drink too much, Mom would get upset, and we would hurry out the door or retreat to our room. I knew those events would inform my nighttime symphonies, more along the lines of Mahler's morose Ninth Symphony than Mozart's *The Marriage of Figaro*. That's not to say there weren't any opportunities for uplifting Mozart-like compositions, but they were much less common as my father continued his downward spiral. The mood of the house on any given day seemed to directly inform the timbre and tone of my nighttime concerts.

Keeping a tidy house was not everyone's priority, but my mother never failed to follow her oft-repeated belief, "You can be poor and still be clean." She was always washing and scrubbing, and even performing makeshift home repairs. She fixed up holes in the wall to keep the rodents out.

The crafty vermin weren't the only critters we were battling. Cockroaches thrived all over the city but especially in low-income New Jersey communities. Every night was like Mardi Gras for those slimy monsters: one big creepy-crawly party. They found their way into our shoes and clothes, hid in the kitchen cabinets and garbage cans, and even managed to wriggle into the refrigerator. My mother waged a never-ending battle with the dark creatures, some so big they cast their own shadow. She had traced the root cause of the infestation to our less-fastidious neighbors. Since they were unfazed by the degenerate intruders, she was forever spraying pesticides, careful to rotate brands before the wily pests could build up a tolerance.

My grandmother was a maid in Fort Lee. She was a very fair-skinned Black woman, and people would say she looked Native American or Latin. Sometimes, she brought home food, like pies, and even clothing that the children of the families she worked for had outgrown or just didn't like. I was often in awe of the stories my grandmother told. She was born in Maryland in 1898 and saw the unspeakable horrors of White supremacy on a daily basis. Eventually she settled back in Maryland, but she said, "I'll never go to western Maryland. That's where it all happened. I can still hear the sound of Confederate soldiers, the evil spirits that haunt the dark woods."

When boys in the neighborhood were around ten or eleven years old, we hung around outside the Universal Supermarket on Bergen Avenue. The store was located in the more affluent area of town, so folks walked there to do their shopping and then walked back home. We meandered around in the parking lot to ask White folks if we could carry their shopping bags home for them. If they said yes, we loaded the groceries into makeshift carts and even helped take them inside their beautiful houses or apartments. Even as a young boy, I marveled at the marble entranceways and fine wood furnishings. Once the job was completed, our customers gave us a quarter or maybe fifty cents, and back we went to the market in search of our next prospect.

Sometimes, my younger brother, Michael, shined shoes, and I joined in if I couldn't find any grocery shoppers to assist. Had our mother found out what we were up to, she would have put a stop to it real fast. She did not think it was dignified, particularly the shoeshines, but it didn't bother us one bit, because all we wanted to do was earn a little money as a way of trying to help the family.

My mother was notoriously frugal. We were used to eating grits every day, because they could feed the whole family. In December she would take a house plant and cover it with homemade decorations for our Christmas tree. I never had a birthday party, school pictures, or anything like that. If we were lucky, we got clothes from John's

Bargain Store or J. M. Fields in Jersey City. The clothes invariably faded after a couple washes, and the insides of the shoes popped right out. Sometimes, my dad bought "dead man shoes," which were old, usually oversized combat boots that were sold after someone had passed away.

One time, a number of us kids decided that we wanted to join the Cub Scouts. The only problem was that we couldn't afford to buy the uniforms, and every kid knows the uniform is an important part of the Scouts. Necessity being the mother of invention, one of the older boys came up with a solution. "Why not make our own shirts and shorts by using the upholstery from the old sofas in the back field?" Had the pattern been closer to regulation blue, the idea might have worked.

Every weekend, the parks in Jersey City and New York exuded palpable energy, and the diverse rhythms were an unparalleled breeding ground for creativity. You could feel it in the cadence of an old man walking down the street, the hat on his head tilted slightly to the side. You heard it in the hum of conversations and the sounds of impromptu concerts as people of all races and backgrounds danced and sang along. On Sundays, beautiful harmonies wafted from open church windows as the voices of gospel singers mingled with the distinctive sounds of the bongo players on the grass. It was always marvelous, irresistible fun.

It was not hard to find creative inspiration. The din that spilled from the rib joints, bars, and clubs out onto the street quite often came from struggling artists who eventually gained enough acclaim to travel beyond the confines of our neighborhood. Many of the greats either resided in the area or frequently passed through, since we were only a short subway ride from Manhattan. Out of our neighborhood came the hugely popular comedian Flip Wilson ("The devil made me do it"); 1950s pop and R&B star Roy Hamilton; 1960s vocal groups the Duprees, the Manhattans, and the Spellbinders; and much later, the Grammy Award–winning hip-hop group Naughty by Nature.

The legendary soul, blues, and R&B performers of that era played live shows at the Monticello Theater down the street. It was your typical Black community theater that doubled as a movie theater when there were no live shows scheduled. The seats were dirty and the floors sticky—a real haven for our cockroach friends. Undeterred, my brother, sister, and I regularly spent entire Saturdays there watching cartoons and then maybe a horror feature; that is, unless there was a "turn out" with a bunch of kids fighting and tearing up the place.

Legend had it that during one of the stage shows, some of the ruffians managed to detach the upstairs concession stand and toss it over the balcony railing. Supposedly that "turn out" was the last straw, and as a consequence, entertainment came to an official halt at the Monticello. Soon thereafter, in an act of instant karma or divine providence, the theater was converted into a church.

Our move from Ingwersen Place to a tenement at 46 Storms Avenue marked a small but meaningful shift in our quality of life. We had graduated to a standard of living that at least fast-forwarded us to the beginning of the twentieth century. Still no hot water or central heating, but at least we had an electric heater and our own telephone line, and the move was indirectly made possible by me.

At age thirteen I'd found a job delivering the *Jersey Journal* after school and on weekends. Then I picked up a route to also deliver the Newark-based *Star-Ledger*. I worked seven days a week to serve over four hundred homes as a way to earn some money. It was in one of those papers I delivered that my mother read an ad about a job training program. Soon she was learning how to be a keypunch operator, cutting-edge technology at the time and a much better-paying job than her previous stint sorting neckties at the garment factory.

My best friend, Ricky Westfield, also lived on Storms Avenue. Ricky already had this big personality, and people gravitated toward him like bees to honey, because he was not only charismatic but also a genuinely open, warm, and caring guy. The way he looked when he walked into a room also made a huge impression. He was tall, like me, and less muscular, but he had a style all his own. He took to wearing boots that made him look even taller. In the 1960s he had this Jimi Hendrix/Sly Stone look—tie-dye shirts, bell-bottomed trousers, and a wild Afro.

Personality-wise, I was more cautious and focused, more of an introvert, and definitely much slower in learning the ways of the world. Ricky was the risk taker, a street-smart kid. From a young age, he hung out with the older guys who showed him the ropes. He did what he wanted to do and took things right to the edge. It showed itself in simple things like driving faster than the speed limit or getting involved with girls he had no business being with.

He had no trouble speaking his mind, which could make things really interesting at times. Before we would head out on an adventure, he frequently taunted me with a devilish grin: "You know what's going to happen to us tonight?" He helped me open up and become more outgoing, and I showed him that sometimes slow and steady wins the race. We complemented each other very well.

Ricky also loved music, and that was a common bond between us. He was interested in the piano, and I'd shared my ideas of possibly playing the drums in a band. Throughout my childhood I was forever tapping on plates and cups with butter knives and spoons. I found that if I hit a surface with the slightest change in force, I could manipulate the sound it created. Soon I was able to mimic tunes I'd heard in my head at night or songs that came on our transistor radio, and that fed my desire to get a real drum set. Ricky and I had endless discussions about how we could make amazing music like Stevie Wonder and Sly Stone.

Our families were close, and they used to call me "Beat" and Ricky "Music" because of our shared interest, but there were plenty of doubters. They'd say, "You're not going to make it in music. We're

going to be NBA stars, and you two might be able to play in the band
at our halftime."

Around that time my parents separated, mostly due to my father's
aggressive behavior and excessive drinking. If I said, "Dad, can I have
a quarter?" he'd say, "You're eating, ain't you?" When he was drinking, he was *that* guy.

I know he put up with a lot to provide for us, dealing with coal
dust going down his throat all day, probably developing black lung
disease or worse. He was also dealing with internal demons that none
of us truly understood, especially my mother. I guess she grew tired
of the never-ending cycle of self-destruction, and to be honest, it was
a sigh of relief for the rest of us. Because I was the oldest, it became
my responsibility to look out for my brother and sister while Mom
worked at her new keypunch job.

Thanks to the money from my newspaper delivery route and my
mother's new job, I was able to start assembling a makeshift drum
set. After much pleading, my mother had finally agreed to buy me a
beat-up bass drum that I'd seen at a pawn shop downtown for fourteen dollars. With my savings, I bought a snare with a plastic shell
from the local music shop. Then I borrowed a floor tom-tom that
had no pedal or skins; only the white cardboard remained. I balanced
the cymbal on a wire hanger attached to an aluminum rod that was
jammed into the base of the tom-tom. If being a dirt-poor, inner-city
kid had taught me anything, it was that I had to be resourceful.

In our basement among the leaky pipes and smell of sewage, I
gingerly balanced that piecemeal drum set in front of a concrete block
that I used as a seat. I spent all of my free time pounding away on
those drums. Every time the drum set fell apart, I reassembled it and
started again. When I was finally able to coax out a decent facsimile
of a familiar song, I realized that if I could create sound with that, I
could play almost anything!

To pursue my dream, I decided that I needed lessons from a pro. I found a local teacher named Joe. He'd played drums with the Shirelles, a New Jersey group that was one of the first to make it big with hits like "Baby It's You," "Will You Love Me Tomorrow," and "Mama Said." Joe was encouraging from the start. When I sat down to play for him so he could assess my ability, he quickly said, "Wow, you're a natural!"

The lessons were three dollars each, and I knew my mother couldn't afford that. I had six dollars to spend and asked Joe to teach me as much as he could in two lessons. Joe understood and quickly showed me the basics: whole notes, quarter notes, sixteenth notes, rolls, flams, drags, paradiddles, and so on. It was a lot of information coming at me quickly, but I absorbed as much as I could. At the end of our second lesson, he recommended a book called *Modern Interpretation of Snare Drum Rudiments* by an amazing drummer named Buddy Rich, who started out as a young kid in vaudeville. (Much later, Joe even came to one of the Kool & the Gang concerts.)

Once I had enough money saved, I went back to the music store and bought that book. I pored over each page and studied the solos and music patterns over and over until I could reproduce them on my tattered drum set.

Every day, from the time I got out of school until late at night, I played the drums in that basement while ignoring the broken glass, leaky pipes, and foul stench of sewage. Our neighbors in the building knew what I was doing, and I couldn't believe no one ever complained about the noise I was making. Not a single person ever said to my mother, "Mrs. Brown, can you stop that boy from making such a racket?"

All the neighborhood kids went to the same elementary school, PS18, where I was on the track team with my friends. The coach said, "Why do you want to be in music? You can get a scholarship in track, George. You're never going to make it in music anyway." Though I enjoyed track, hearing those doubts over and over only helped to fuel my passion.

By the time I was ready for sixth grade, they decided to divide our class among several junior high schools around the city. I was one of the few assigned to PS11, which was 99.9 percent White. At least there were three other Black students at the school, so, including me, that made two girls and two boys. Naturally, we gravitated to each other and often wondered aloud why we'd been yanked from our familiar neighborhoods and placed in such a different type of school. Being thrown into such a situation gave the four of us a strong bond and a lifelong friendship.

The curriculum was completely foreign to us. The subjects were nothing like ones we were used to. Of course, I was also the only minority on the track team. When I'd return to my neighborhood, I was back in familiar territory, but straddling the two cultures took some getting used to.

Looking back on those developmental years, I marvel at how things came together in ways that seem nothing short of miraculous. Life can feel at any time to be an exercise in randomness, but what unfolded hardly feels accidental. No doubt our sense of purpose, our passion, and our hard work kept us on a defined path and created its own momentum. One thing led to another. Even experiences that might have been seen as devastating adversity at the time turned out to have hidden blessings. Special people came into our lives at just the right time.

On New Year's Eve 1964, I saw Ricky coming down Storms Avenue with two guys playing trumpets. As the trio approached, the new guys were blowing "Auld Lang Syne" on their horns, and the sounds grew louder as they came closer. I wasn't sure what to think, but I loved the spectacle of it all. Ricky must have told them I played drums, because when they saw me, one of them shouted, "Hey, go up on the roof and play the drums for us. We'll keep playing our trumpets and walking toward downtown to see if we can still hear each other."

I said, "OK, I'll do that, but I don't know if you're gonna hear me."

Then we all stared at each other and burst out laughing at our silly idea. Ricky introduced them as Ronnie Bell and Robert "Spike" Mickens. He'd met them while listening to records at the home of Buddy Mays, a jazz aficionado who lived in the neighborhood. The four of us hit it off immediately, forming an instant bond sealed by our mutual love of music. I wasn't sure what the future had in store for us, but I was eager to find out.

Soul Town

I firmly believe that nothing happens by mistake. Call it divine intervention if you wish, but it seems that people come into our lives for a specific reason. Not all of them are meant to go the distance, but some are. Especially in those relationships that end up spanning several decades, there are problems that arise, big and small. It's going to happen. It can be difficult navigating those issues, but I've found that it's usually worth the effort, especially with the people you want to keep in your life. When those connections are particularly secure, it's more than just a friendship. It's a shared spirituality that is even stronger when it's rooted in creativity and imagination.

Creativity, turning ideas into reality, is such an elusive and mysterious concept, an ability that is often born of conflict or challenging situations. Sometimes, it's a way of viewing the world in a new way, a way far different from everyday reality. I think that's what I was doing with those nighttime symphonies I created in my head. It wasn't so much an escape from my reality as a glimpse into the limitless possibilities that lay ahead if I followed my passion.

Having creativity fuel your very existence is uncommon, and finding others who share your aesthetic is as rare as a shooting star in the night sky. But when you find those people, when you connect with others who share your passion for creativity and innovation, it's important to realize that they were put in your life for a reason. It's up to you whether you work to keep them in your life or let them drift away. That might sound heavy coming from a kid growing up in a New Jersey row house, but I spent a lot of time thinking about my future and dreaming about the possibilities, all in the hopes of manifesting a life full of unlimited opportunity. I had the dreamer's disease, and the only cure was success.

Ricky Westfield was not just my best buddy; because he was my neighbor, our mothers were friends as well. As single parents they looked out for each other, and even though we didn't have a lot of money, my mom even bought Ricky an electric piano at one point. It was a pink Wurlitzer like the ones Stevie Wonder and Sly Stone used to play.

After I met the other guys through Ricky, I found out that Spike lived in Lafayette Gardens, and Ronnie and his brother Robert "Kool" Bell were not far away in the Montgomery Gardens public housing complex, a high-rise apartment building built in 1957 with federal funds. What started as a viable option for low-income families became run-down and plagued with crime as the years rolled on. Even the smallest details mirrored bleakness, like how the door to the elevator reminded me of a solitary confinement jail cell. It had a little window of iron mesh instead of glass, but that didn't really matter, because the elevators never worked anyway. We used the stairways that always greeted us with the unforgettable, stinging stench of urine.

The seventh-floor hallway at Montgomery, where the Bell brothers lived, was always dark, because addicts had a habit of knocking out the light bulbs so they could shoot up in semi-privacy. Once, I stumbled into a guy who was cooking his concoction in the shadows, the metal spoon glowing red as he prepared to temporarily escape the physical world. It was my good fortune that not a speck of his precious potion was spilled. Otherwise I would have been on the receiving end of a junkie's rage.

As teenagers we made the best of our circumstances and got into a bit of mischief, or "devilment," as my grandmother called it. There was a marshy piece of land across from Montgomery Gardens that folks used as a dump. One day we looked over there and saw a gray coffin floating in the stagnant water that seeped from a nearby lake. Not having any better options at the time, we spent the day investigating the macabre marshlands. Then Ricky and I headed back to our neighborhood, where I spent the rest of my free time practicing the drums.

A man named Danny Austin regularly walked past our house on his way home after coming from the city on the metro. I'd be banging on drums in the basement, and he'd stop to talk to my mother any time she was sitting on our porch stoop. It was clear to me that he was flirting with her, and maybe she enjoyed the attention. He was a member of a fledgling doo-wop group from nearby Bayonne called the Ad Libs. They had a hit with the song "The Boy from New York City" before the Manhattan Transfer came along.

One day I watched as he hoisted a drum set into the back of a wood-paneled station wagon before heading to a gig. Then he yelled over, "Hey, Georgie, we're gonna take you on the road with us!"

I was so excited that I ran into the house. This was it! My dream was coming true! I caught my breath and blurted to Mama, "They gonna take me on the road!"

She gave me that look of hers and said, "They not taking you on the road, boy. You're twelve years old!"

At one point our family converted to the Episcopal denomination. I'm not sure what prompted the change, but like a good son, I went along with it. Every Sunday we took a short walk down the street to the Church of the Incarnation. The congregation was formed in 1910, because African Americans were denied entry to other Episcopalian churches in the area. Being an altar boy proved a great advantage, because Father Avery allowed me to go into the parish house where he lived so I could practice the piano. It was located downstairs, under the church. There was a long, rectangular hallway with the piano parked against a wall. If the door was locked, I would knock gently, hoping he was there.

When he opened the door, I'd ask, "Father, may I play the piano today?"

He always said yes. I'm sure he could tell that there was a lot of music inside of me that needed to get out. Plus, he was providing a creative outlet to ensure that I wasn't roaming around the neighborhood. He could have easily turned me down, but fortunately, he did not. Talk about divine intervention. Father Avery was a true angel and my musical salvation when I needed it. There would be no devilment for me.

Ricky, Spike, Ronnie, and Kool had started a little group called the Jazziacs. One day I ran into them on the sidewalk, and they had their instruments with them.

"What's up?" I asked.

"We were going to go play up at Buddy Mays's place, but it was called off," one of them said.

"Yeah, our drummer couldn't make it. Not sure he's committed to music like we are," said another.

"You could play in the basement of my church," I told them. "Why don't we head over there and try a song or two?"

There in the parish hall, the four of them started playing their instruments while I jumped on the drums. We messed around with a jazz tune called "Take Five," and it was amazing. Our playing wasn't perfect; there's no denying it was raw. Hell, we were all of fourteen years old. Yet I could feel that something was there. I think we all felt it. We fell into the same groove effortlessly, and I picked up the beat right away, adjusting the tempo without saying a word. It felt not only good but also natural.

After we finished, none of us spoke. We waited for the music to slowly fade away. Then we headed back outside, and I went across the street to Mr. Green's Candy Shop to buy some gumdrops. I looked up to find Ronnie right in front of me.

"Would you like to be our drummer?" he asked.

"Sure," I said, trying to act casual when I was bursting inside.

At only fourteen, things were already beginning to snowball! Before long we were playing small gigs. I got along with all the guys, and we learned a lot from each other. Ronnie brought that indispensable quality of pure discipline, no nonsense, and no compromise on quality. He challenged us to aim for a higher standard. He also stressed that we had to know our worth: "Unless we're getting paid, we're not going."

Ronnie could also express his playfulness through his sax. In our teenage years, we might be performing a folk song when all of a sudden he would break into a John Coltrane solo. To him, Coltrane was the god of the saxophone.

"Turn that noise off," his mother would yell at him from the other room when he was at home practicing along with a recording. She had an appreciation for Ronnie, but to her it must have sounded like a herd of charging elephants. But he was mastering the complex and challenging chord changes Coltrane had pioneered. As time went on and he developed as a musician, Ronnie learned how to consider what the audience wanted to hear and still stay within the melody. As a drummer I loved when he went to that spontaneous, off-the-charts space, because it challenged me to keep up.

Ricky was always right there cutting up most of the time. We were like the Three Stooges when we hung out together. We always had that chemistry.

I found Spike to be one of the most intriguing and fascinating characters in the band. It was abundantly clear from our first meeting that he was a true genius. I could see the wheels turning when he played, and he was clearly possessed by the music. That word *genius* is so overused that it sounds like a cliché, but he was the epitome. His father was a trumpet player, and his older brother, Butch, was also a fine jazz musician. So, surrounded by such influence, he became a walking encyclopedia of jazz history.

Spike's brilliance came from a form of eccentricity that was lovable, colorful, and sure to keep everyone around him on their toes. Like the famous picture of an older Albert Einstein riding on a bicycle with his wild white hair, Spike's appearance and demeanor made a lasting impression. Imagine this: a straw Mexican sombrero, a big black beard, a jumpsuit that was one of the costumes he wore onstage, and an oversized boom box that seemed permanently attached to his shoulder.

Day in and day out, that's how he looked for years. That was his uniform. He didn't care one bit about fame or the trappings of success. It was all about playing music. He could walk through a neighborhood with his boom box, find a barbecue, and just invite himself in, smoking his Kool cigarettes and drinking a beer. Nobody ever seemed to mind. He made friends with enviable ease.

Even later, when Kool & the Gang was a success, the material things didn't seem to matter to him—not the platinum records, the number-one hits, the awards, the appearances on big television shows. None of that mattered. "Spike, why don't you buy a condo?" I would ask him. But he preferred his little apartment above a bar on a side street in Jersey City. "No, I like the community," he'd say. No matter where he traveled in the world, Spike wandered around and found his "community." People would come backstage and say, "Oh, we know Spike. He came to one of our parties."

After Kool & the Gang achieved worldwide fame, we usually stayed at five-star hotels on tour as a treat to ourselves—the Four Seasons, the Ritz-Carlton, St. Regis, and so on. Wearing his beat-up sombrero and jumpsuit, Spike invariably found his way to the bar to mingle with the posh set of executives and well-heeled socialites. On occasion he would even crank up his boom box to drown out the bar's ambient music.

He especially loved to play Steely Dan, his favorite group. He appreciated their hybrid of pop tinged with jazz and the innovative harmonies and chord changes. When someone invariably asked him, "Could you please turn that down?" he would smile and crank it up. Since the hotel was well aware of its VIP guest's antics, a call would be made to our road manager, who would come storming down from his room to intervene. Other times, Spike might sit down at the piano or clavier if there was one in the bar. "Cha, cha, chachacha, cha, cha, chachacha," he'd sing. "Listen to the birds." He always said that all the rhythms and sounds and music came primordially from animals.

So when the guys asked me to join the group now called the Jazz Birds, I couldn't believe my luck. My dream was coming true. I didn't have unrealistic expectations that we would perform on huge stages or anything; I was just excited to play drums in a band. Plus, I got to hang out with my friends, and that made the new experiences easier to navigate for my introverted, younger self. We were soon playing at local dances and socials, and even the coffeehouses of Jersey City. The gigs gradually expanded into New York City, which meant we had to take the subway. Fortunately, our parents allowed us to go, despite the fact that we were just teenagers, because in their minds it was right down the street. It helped that Ronnie and his brother Kool also had family up on Sixty-Fifth Street, including Kool's godfather, the amazing jazz pianist and composer Thelonious Monk.

Whether good timing or pure luck, there was no shortage of venues to play, especially for performers who showed up on time and did a good job entertaining the crowd. It was a time when live music was everywhere. Of course, with no Internet or, for most folks, cable TV, live performance was the only way to see a new act. I was amazed that somehow word got out each time we played a gig, and that led to another one and another one.

The Jazz Birds even played amateur night at the Apollo Theater a few times, placing third once and receiving an honorable mention from the venerable MC Charles "Honi" Coles, a tap-dancing legend and close friend of Billy Strayhorn, Duke Ellington's legendary arranger, composer, and pianist.

"Ladies and gentlemen, you're going to hear a lot from these young men in the future," Coles told the audience after we finished our performance of one of Ricky's compositions, called "Dugi" (a street term for heroin). Jazz music was a harder sell at those shows and, of course, the competition was intense. It was a far less risky proposition for groups to follow the hot music forms of the time: the emerging Motown sound, the Atlantic Records sound (Aretha Franklin), the Memphis sound (Otis Redding, the Bar-Kays, Booker T. & the M.G.'s), and the West Coast sound (Sly and the Family Stone). Instead, we were doing a mix of standards and some original compositions. We also played the Jazzmobile, which put on concerts all around the greater metropolitan area to promote "America's classical music."

Having opportunities was amazing, but soon the pressure was intense. It meant we had to deliver to keep getting gigs, and sometimes, the greatest obstacle was our own fear. On one occasion, Butch Mickens, a mentor to us, asked me to fill in on drums with the group the Jazziacs for a performance at a festival in Harlem. The Jazziacs led by example, and we learned a lot from them. The drummer, Ronald Cherry, had taught me so much about timing and stamina, but he was in the Marines and serving in Vietnam. The war put on hold the careers of so many great talents, and sadly a large percentage of them never got that part of their lives back on track when they returned.

The group's backup drummer, Vincent Hall, couldn't make the show for some reason, so I was chosen. Being on the same stage with such great musicians for the first time was a defining moment. I was a bundle of nerves, but I still accepted the challenge. It got intense when the concert promoter was nervous that the young group (which was made up of minors in their late teens) couldn't play up to the standards of the greats who graced the stage that day. Finally, we got to play, and we were scheduled to close the show. The promoter probably thought the audience would have gotten their money's worth by that time, and our performance wouldn't matter too much. But the audience stayed.

Shit, I'm still amazed by our playlist. We did Dizzy Gillespie's "A Night in Tunisia," "Milestones" by Miles Davis, and a few other jazz compositions. The crowd went wild, chanting at us, "Jer-sey boys, Jer-sey boys, Jer-sey boys!" The local jazz radio station even gave me a good review the next morning. At fourteen, it was a highlight in my life and instilled in me greater confidence in my ability as a drummer. I just wished I could hold on to that confidence and avoid the self-doubt that often messed with my head.

When I got back with the Jazz Birds, we started doing little shows at Café Wha? on MacDougal Street in Greenwich Village. The cafe was owned by the father of David Lee Roth of Van Halen fame. It was the club that had launched the careers of 1960s icons like Bob Dylan, Jimi Hendrix, Bruce Springsteen, and Peter, Paul and Mary, not to mention comedians Bill Cosby and Richard Pryor. Richie Havens played there frequently, trying out his new material on the eager beatnik crowd. It was also where we really cut our teeth. Our compensation came in the form of experience and exposure, plus free milkshakes and hamburgers. I was never a big eater, then or now, so I gladly gave my meal to a guy named Junior, who also lived up on Sixty-Fifth. It was a smart move, because in exchange he let me use his drum set for the show so I wouldn't have to drag mine on the subway. It was a good deal for both of us.

Café Wha? was the first gig where Kool played the bass. One of the songs we played with Kool joining on his new instrument was "Comin' Home Baby," a big hit at the time by flutist Herbie Mann. Kool aced that bass, and I could feel the unity among all of us. It felt like we were elevating our showmanship to a new level. Things were coming together for us, and it felt so natural. Kool was no stranger to music, that's for sure. He was good at playing the cello in high school. His father, Robert "Bobby" Bell, was a top-ten-ranked professional featherweight boxer who had a certain calmness that balanced him out. Those traits were unmistakable in his son as well, and that explained the nickname.

What was so impressive about Kool from the outset was his proficiency, and how he played with such confidence. Sometimes with a guitar or bass, a novice can hit a chord and it goes *thunk*, because the fingers have put improper pressure on the strings. He never did that. As time went on, Kool quickly developed his own style, and with it, a growing recognition as one of the greats. The jazz bassist Jaco Pastorius (best known for his innovation with the group Weather Report and in his solo work) used to frequently come to our recording sessions just to hang out and watch Kool play.

When we first started booking gigs, Kool would sometimes not show up for rehearsals. He chose to hang out with his friends instead. At the time he was still part of a street gang called the Adventures. It had started as a social club for the older members, but the younger ones were definitely bangers. Those kids were trouble, but nothing compared to the intense gang culture that came along years later. Nevertheless, they were known to carry knives and zip guns, toss an occasional Molotov cocktail, and drop objects off rooftops to scare the oblivious pedestrians on the sidewalk below.

Ronnie told me he was out with Kool one night during that period, and one of the gang members chased after him with a hatchet. "If this is what it's like when you hang out with these guys, that's it for me," he told Kool.

I had an encounter myself around that time with Eagle, the leader of the Adventures. I came downtown to see Ronald when he and Kool lived over a bar, the same bar where we had started rehearsing. As far as the gang was concerned, downtown, midtown, and uptown were rival territories. So I was a midtown guy going downtown, and that meant I was fair game. Eagle started challenging me. I'm no fighter, so I wasn't sure what to do, but I grabbed a nearby bicycle and began swinging it in his direction. That was out of character for a quiet kid like me, but I knew that it was important to stand my ground, especially against the leader of the group. Fortunately, it worked. From that moment forward, I got lots of respect from him because I didn't back down. I had earned a free pass from the Adventures.

Sometime later Eagle was drafted and sent to Vietnam to become a paratrooper. He came back to New Jersey a wounded vet, describing to me in detail how he had been hit by a bullet while parachuting, and it had gone through his leg before striking another guy.

The Jazz Birds made another big move, but it was just down the street. My mother had decided to change churches to the larger St. John's Episcopal, because it had more community programs and outreach activities, especially in the parish hall. Just like Father Avery before him, Father Castle allowed us to practice our music there to take advantage of the beautiful acoustics.

The huge hall was called the Ankh, after the Egyptian sign for life, a cross with a large loop at its head that is also sometimes used as a symbol in Catholic churches. St. John's organized jazz concerts and dances there, and we frequently played. Any money we made went straight to buying better-quality instruments to improve our performance. Through the experience, we all became much more versatile musicians. The place was packed with so many young people that the walls seemed like they were sweating. We played our normal jazz repertory but mixed in the Motown stuff that most of the kids around us listened to at that time. Of course, in the process we had no idea that we were taking baby steps toward the funky fusion sound we would become known for all over the world.

Fortuitously, the Ankh was also the practice hall and gathering spot for other musicians who were making waves in the world of music. One of the bands had Pharoah Sanders on alto saxophone, John Lewis on piano, James Taylor on tenor saxophone, and Billy Hart on drums. They often took the time to sit and talk to us, and sometimes, they let us practice with them. I will never forget the vision of watching Pharoah show thirteen-year-old Ronnie how to clean his pads. Here was this man regarded as one of the best alto sax players in the world, dunking Ronnie's saxophone in a sink of water like some baptismal rite of passage. Mentoring often becomes a natural, reflexive act when older musicians recognize budding talent, and that's what was happening. They were just passing along what another elder had probably done for them when they were young and starting out—the continuation of a beautiful musical legacy.

I had been able to transfer back to our neighborhood to attend Lincoln High School. One day, when I was beginning the ninth grade, I walked through the auditorium on my way to algebra class and was stopped in the hallway by a stocky guy I didn't know.

"I hear that you play drums," he said to me, with no discernable expression on his face.

I quickly sized him up and said, "Um, yes."

Then he told me that he lived directly across the street from my grandparents, my mother's brother, and their large family. He also asked me if I knew a piano player, because he was planning a recording session. I recommended Ricky Westfield.

I found out his name was Claydes Smith, a very talented young guitarist. As a youth he spent his time studying the albums of guitarist Wes Montgomery. Those octaves he played so smoothly, so melodically, and with such great fluidity showed Montgomery's influence.

Claydes was laid-back, but when he played the guitar, he came to life! He was totally obsessed. His passion was like a runaway locomotive. He was also a great person to have in your corner. He was outspoken and quick to jump to your defense if someone in the studio was getting out of line or coming down hard on a fellow musician. If one of the guys gave him a disapproving look when he made a mistake, Claydes glared back, obstinately playing the same sour note over and over again with a "What do you think about that?" attitude. It was not from arrogance. Rather, it was his way of saying, "You don't need to correct me. I know what I'm doing. Everyone makes mistakes. That means you too."

We made a date for the three of us to get together and practice. Next we went to a studio in Newark to record. Claydes Smith and the Rhythms cut one track, a blues song with a shuffle beat. His father paid for the session, because he believed so much in his son's future. His instincts were on point. Our very first hit single, aptly titled "Kool & the Gang," was born from a guitar lick Claydes had created. When a record producer somewhere in the world says, "Give me that Kool & the Gang groove," they are talking about Claydes Smith and his artistry.

Not long after, Claydes stopped me in the school hallway again as we were changing from homeroom to the first-period class we also shared.

"Do you know any other musicians?" he asked. "There's this guy named Donald Key. He is starting an organization called the Soul Town Revue." Claydes went on to explain that Key was trying to replicate what Berry Gordy had done in Detroit with Motown.

"Yes, I know a few guys," I answered. In no time Ronald Bell, Spike Mickens, Robert "Kool" Bell, and I joined the group called the Soul Town Revue.

We started rehearsing at St. John's, and we clicked as brothers from the beginning. Then Dennis Thomas agreed to join us. He had previously been the flutist and percussionist with Five Sounds, Butch Mickens' group. He preferred to hang with the older guys even though he was a couple of years younger than the rest of us. But when he decided to play with us, he added the alto sax to his musical arsenal. As valedictorian of his elementary school, Dennis proved to be the intellectual of our group and a man of few words.

The Soul Town Revue turned out to be the best musical training we could ever have hoped for. Donald Key got us a gig at the Canyon Club in Bayonne, and we set up shop as the house band. Every night we pumped out soul, blues, R&B, pop, and funk with heavy inspiration from Sly and the Family Stone and James Brown.

One summer night after a packed performance at the Kenya Club, I missed my ride back to Jersey City. I couldn't bring an entire drum set on the city bus, so I found an abandoned shopping cart, loaded my set into it, and walked seven miles to get home. It took a few hours, and I even stopped once to pick a few ripe peaches from overhanging tree branches along my path.

I sometimes think back to that night. The image of that solitary young man pushing a wobbly shopping cart packed with a rattling drum kit through the yellow-tinged darkness. There was no anger or regret, but a more expansive surrender to the circumstances that allowed me to treat that long walk as an adventure. My life became far more complex in the following months and years as my world expanded and my career exploded.

I understand with gratitude how that walk has been replayed in various forms throughout my life as I have navigated through challenges, adversities, opportunities, and accomplishments. The ability to be that solitary walker in my spirit has truly helped me better separate truth from illusion.

The Gene Redd School

Gene Redd Jr. sat down with us at a rehearsal spot on Stegman Street up on what Jersey City locals would call the Hill, because it had a slightly higher elevation. Gene's father was Clarence Redd, an accomplished trumpet player and a member of several bands in the 1940s and '50s, including those of Cootie Williams and Earl Bostic. He also played with many of the greats, like John Coltrane, and later joined James Brown's band. His recordings included "I Want to Take You Higher," "Pneumonia," and "Please Come Home for Christmas." With music in his DNA, Gene was a producer for an independent record label called De-Lite, and he was on the lookout for a band that would put the label on the map. He was sure we were it.

At the time, we were managed by Jerome Gasper, who worked on the Domenico Bus Service. After telling us how he thought our sound was "cutting edge," Gene said, "I don't have limos and I don't know any buses, but what I do have is a knowledge of the record business. I know how to produce quality recordings, and I know a hit song when I hear it." He wanted to sign us to De-Lite and asked us to decide right then and there. We went into the next room and talked it over. His confidence in us and his ambition to make it in the business won us over. We quickly agreed to go with Gene. We were ready to be shot into the musical stratosphere . . . or at least cut a song or two.

But nothing happened for weeks. And those weeks turned into months. We were all frustrated by the inaction from someone who seemed so motivated when we signed. Finally, I decided to see what was up. I rode the subway to his neighborhood and found his house on Jerome Avenue. I walked up to the door and gave a strong knock. I was here for business.

Gene answered and couldn't have been nicer. He even offered me a tuna fish sandwich and asked if we were ready to record. *Ready?*

I told him, "Yes, of course!" The delay could have been a ploy, not unlike how martial arts or masters of higher consciousness test the motivation and passion of their students. At such a young age, I didn't give it too much thought. I just wanted to play my music.

Within days he got us set up at the Ankh, and we began rehearsing. We eventually recorded a song and agreed to retitle it "Chocolate Buttermilk." A disc jockey named Hal Atkins from radio station WWRL was in the studio checking us out at Gene's request. "You guys are great, but remember this," he said. "In this business, you can be up on Monday and back in the car on Friday." We all understood that possibility, but we did not allow it to affect the goal we had set for ourselves.

Gene gave us probably the best advice of all, which we took to heart and put into practice. "You can write for your city. You can write for your region. You can write for your country. But writing for the whole world is the real challenge."

As he put it, we were now "going to the Gene Redd School." It was a one-man show, and Gene acted as his own A&R (artists and repertoire) department to groom groups into making the crucial transition from local recording artists to the big time. His advice continued, and I hung on every word. He encouraged us to think big. "Buy the suit." "Wear this watch." "Show business is all perception."

He recognized that we were some young guys with a fresh sound and a compelling concept. His goal was to bring it all together in a way that made audiences want to be part of the experience. Some suggestions were specific, others less so. It's at that point that we decided that going forward, we would be known as Kool & the Gang. He helped us build on our ideas and talent by bringing out the best in each of us. He suggested that we wear caps like the Delfonics did and add choreography like the Temptations when they glided smoothly across the stage. Maybe the horns could add a step and turn around during some of the songs. The bass guitar could make motions to literally spell out K-O-O-L-A-N-D-T-H-E-G-A-N-G.

Since we'd agreed to work with him, we were all in when it came to his ideas—at least most of them. But we also wanted to see results . . . and we did. As musicians our focus was always on our art, honing our skills with our instruments, and obviously that was time well spent, because we had become even more musically proficient. However, in the Gene Redd School, we realized that we needed more than just talent. We'd been practicing, rehearsing our moves, and focusing on making our performance a true spectacle. We no longer just wanted the audience to hear us; we wanted them to watch us put on a show.

Once Gene thought we were ready, he made an announcement: "Kool & the Gang has a gig at the Apollo." Of course, our group was familiar with the iconic Apollo Theater. We'd played there as the Jazz Birds to a less-than-enthusiastic crowd. We didn't bomb, but we weren't showmen like the other groups. We were straight-up musicians. We were jazz purists (even at a young age) and didn't understand the performance aspect of a live show. So I had a little anxiety about going back; I remembered some of the amazing talent we saw there. I knew we had to bring it, because that audience accepts nothing but the best.

The night of the show, I still wasn't sure how we would be received, but it was now or never. Being the center of attention was never my thing, but I knew it was important to go out and show out. It was time to put all that work into action, and that's what we did. We made that audience feel the funk and understand exactly who Kool & the Gang were—and still are. I put everything into my drums and kept my focus on the audience. We looked sharp, worked the stage, and made sure our playing was top-notch. The audience jumped to their feet and rewarded us with a standing ovation. We were on our way.

Gene had his own private record label called Red Coach, and he put out our song, called "Kool & the Gang." The song didn't go anywhere, because there was no distribution or marketing. It was frustrating; we were ready to show out and break out. We just needed the opportunity. Then Hal suggested that Gene make a deal with De-Lite Records, since he already had a working relationship with them. So with Gene as the producer, De-Lite released our single "Kool & the Gang" (written by our group) with "Raw Hamburger" (by Gene Redd) on the B-side.

On July 3, 1969, I was walking down Garfield Avenue with my high school girlfriend (and soon-to-be wife) from her after-school job at the Royaltone photo processing lab. I had a little transistor radio in my hand tuned to WWRL when I heard that unmistakable Claydes Smith guitar riff shoot through that staticky little speaker.

The moment I heard that song on the radio, life as I knew it would never be the same. The record went to number two on the rotation and soon cracked the *Billboard* Hot 100 charts at number thirty with a bullet (denoting a fast-moving record). Even though our horn-driven funk song was an instrumental, it was a hit for us and the fledgling record label. It also impressively showcased our talent as musicians, and it still holds up today.

Gene continued to guide us, and we took his sage words seriously, as evidenced by the song "Chocolate Buttermilk," which was released as the B-side of our 1970 single "Let the Music Take Your Mind" and has been sampled more than fifty times over the years. My drum playing on that tune has been used in songs featuring artists like Eric B. & Rakim, Masters at Work, DJ Pierre, EMF, Prince and the New Power Generation, and DJ Scoobie.

Similar to the Jacksons or any number of musicians who get into the game early on, I look back at those early years and realize that I did not have a typical adolescent experience. For me it was all about playing music. There was little hanging out and goofing off. There were no pickup basketball games or hanging out at the movies. I had a passion that burned deep inside me, and it was impossible to deny.

Yet that wasn't my only motivation. It was deeper and more urgent. There was something else driving me.

My father worked hard to support his family but ultimately fell victim to a lethal combination of alcohol and violence. The death of his mother at an early age was a severe blow, and the Black-on-Black racism he experienced because of his dark skin was a heavy burden. He worked seven days a week with a bad back from carrying sacks of coal. Whenever he had time away from the coal, he was transporting furniture for Al Smith Moving Company. So every day he literally had something heavy on his back.

One Christmas it was clear that we had no money, and none of us expected presents. It just wasn't an option. My father got off work on Christmas Eve and went down to the railway yard, where he talked his way into a job shoveling snow off the tracks. He came home late that night with toys for us kids. Somehow he had found a store that was open and spent all the money he made on gifts. It made such an impression on me, because I'd understood that there would be little celebration. Yet there he was at the door, our own real-life Santa.

Like so many men of his generation, he communicated his pain and frustration in destructive ways. One night he came home all cut up after he had gotten into a fight. The police were soon at the door and started beating him with their nightsticks to the point where they were about to bust his head open. I remember screaming, "Stop hitting my daddy!" but they would not relent. He was so strong that he broke the leather restraining straps that bound his wrists. The police were wary of him and, honestly, so were we when he was in that state.

When I was a baby, my drunken father had accidentally smashed in a part of my skull with his elbow. They couldn't locate a pediatric surgeon in Jersey, and finally, one traveled from Chicago. On a snowy

Christmas Day, that surgeon came to Jersey to perform the life-saving surgery on me, pro bono.

Later my mother shared a story about when my father dropped a cast-iron vent dangerously close to her as she stood by the stove in my grandmother's kitchen. He had also kicked her when she was pregnant with my sister. Years later my father was murdered by acquaintances who poured a deadly overdose of alcohol down his throat to steal the cash he had just won on the numbers.

Despite his checkered history, I always viewed my father with deep love and compassion. I was able to see beyond the drama and tragedy and find the inherent blessings that eventually arose from his efforts to provide for us. That mind-set, that ability to expand my understanding and find positivity in most situations, not only helped me cope with a volatile family life but also made my songwriting even more relatable. It allowed me to see situations from viewpoints other than my own. I learned to reserve judgment and allow the life lessons to inform the music and thereby my consciousness. In music and in life, there is no such thing as failure. Rather, they are a process of continual learning.

My mother and grandmother never doubted that I would be a success, because my birth was a special kind of miracle. Normally, the amniotic sac breaks when a baby is born, but during a *caul* or *en caul* birth, the baby makes a miraculous debut into the world wrapped partially or completely in the bubble of the amniotic sac. That's how I arrived, a gelatinous covering over my face like a heavenly veil of mystery.

That was a sign of predestined greatness, a path out of poverty and into prosperity. My grandmother supported that idea because she was recognized as someone with heightened perception, a second sight, a keen intuition. The first time she saw me, she immediately declared to my mother in a hushed tone, "Eleanora, the child is gifted. He's going to make a name for himself."

My first wife saw the gift as well. As she combed her hair one day, I was standing behind her. She looked at me and started screaming as she dropped her hairbrush.

"What's wrong?" I asked.

She said, "A light just came out of your eye."

"Don't worry about it, baby," I reassured her. "That's the way it is. It happens. You're going to see more of that."

Every once in a while, it still happens, but not as much lately. When my eye twitches, I know it's coming. It's allowed me to see rods of light emanating wherever I go. The other day I was sitting outside looking at a palm tree against the sunny Los Angeles sky, and I saw dozens of tiny bubbles of light dancing in the air.

I watched as they hovered over the palm tree. One moved slowly at first and then *zoom*, it was gone. Other people born with a veil have shared similar stories. One time when living in New York, I walked into my apartment and was greeted by three globes of light the size of basketballs. I went to sleep undeterred. It was a common occurrence at that point.

That might have been what led to my vivid dreams that have often come true, just like the music I visualized into reality. That's why I always felt like I'd be successful. It wasn't out of arrogance but simply something predestined. That's also why I never had a backup plan. There was no need.

As a young musician just going out into the world, I too expected great things.

Who's Going to Take the Weight?

The Chitterling Circuit was made up of clubs, theaters, Black college auditoriums, ballrooms, and Black VFW halls, which were the only places Black performers could play before segregation slowly loosened its ugly grip on society.

As Kool & the Gang, we made our way through the Northeast, South, and Midwest. Traveling on dirt roads around the rural South was an eye-opener for most of us kids from New Jersey, as we packed on the same Greyhound or Trailways bus with the members of other bands, such as the Delfonics and the Chi-Lites. Since we were just beginning to make our name in the industry, we were booked to open for established acts like Gladys Knight & the Pips, the O'Jays, and Wilson Pickett.

Within the circuit there lived an unspoken tradition of gentle mentoring. It was a beautiful rite of passage when artists who had already come into their own would say, "Let me pull your coat," which meant they were willing to give us tips and pointers about the business. The promoter for that tour sent along a man named Mr. Underwood, who collected the performance fees after each show—often loose bills stuffed in a brown paper bag. Motel rooms were always the cheapest we could find, which usually meant they were not the cleanest. Some places even doubled as whorehouses. Meals on the road were at places like Waffle House or skipped altogether if we were running late. The rare stays at a Holiday Inn were the pinnacle of luxury.

With our first R&B chart single, "Kool & the Gang," and later "The Gang's Back Again," getting airplay, the audiences gradually got bigger. As the collective awareness quickly blossomed, I knew my life would never be the same. Ladies began screaming and running up to the stage. That was a completely new and unexpected experience for a quiet kid from Jersey like me. After the shows it was tough just getting to the car, because fans surrounded the vehicle and would not let us go. *Whoa!* This was heavy stuff. Understanding that it happens is one thing, but being in the middle of that sheer and unadulterated delirium is overwhelming. I had never felt anxiety like that, and it was getting worse. It was hard to believe that banging on the drums would land me in such an uncontrolled situation. It was like being shot up into space, weightless and without control.

Musically, we were crushing it. Our self-titled first album came out in 1969. It included our two hit singles along with "Breeze & Soul," "Chocolate Buttermilk," "Sea of Tranquility," "Give It Up," "Since I Lost My Baby," "Kool's Back Again," and "Raw Hamburger." The singles reached number nineteen on the *Billboard* Hot R&B Songs chart. We followed that with two live albums released in 1971: *Live at the Sex Machine* and *Live at PJ's*. In 1972 we put out two more albums: *Music Is the Message*, which went to number twenty-five on the *Billboard* Top R&B Albums chart, and *Good Times*, which peaked at number thirty-four and included a ballad I wrote called "Father, Father."

For the first time in my life, I saw bags full of money circulating throughout the industry. While we were on tour, we received a small cut, because our primary reward was experience and exposure. It was an investment in our musical future. Having a firsthand view of the financial aspects, or lack thereof, made a lasting impression on me. I quickly understood that the money would come and go, so it was important to manage it carefully. It took me some time to incorporate that concept into my life, but the financial seed had been planted. *Save your money, George. Nothing is guaranteed.*

In time I acclimated to the cycle of performance highs followed by the subsequent return to reality, but the unfiltered accolades and unrelating attention from the audiences were a bit of a struggle for me. While it might seem like a young man's dream, it caused me a lot of stress, because it was an unfamiliar situation, and I found it difficult to trust every stranger's intention. It was miles away from growing up with your people and knowing how everyone moves, good or bad, but eventually I got used to the groupie phenomenon and adjusted as it morphed into a part of my daily life. I was even given a rockstar name, George "Funky" Brown, and was ready for stardom, but I made a conscious effort not to compromise my integrity or authenticity for financial gain or chart positions. The focus had to stay on the quality and integrity of the music.

Back in Jersey City, the band was set to rehearse in the basement of a house owned by a well-known drug dealer called Mr. J. Not the smartest idea. Don't try this at home! One day three White cops barged in during one of our rehearsals while we were innocently getting into our groove. I continued to play until I heard, "Stop the goddamned music!" Then one of the guys grabbed my right cymbal between his hands to silence it. "I said stop the goddamn music!" All of us just looked at each other. One of the men asked where Mr. J was, and since we had no idea, we were ordered to empty our pockets.

The leader of the trio held up a baggie filled with some type of powder. "If we find something under the sofa pillow," he said to us, "who's going to take the weight?" One of the men took the drugs and smiled as he dramatically placed the baggie under a pillow and then pretended that he had just found it. "Look what I found here," he said. "Who's going to take the weight for this?"

We were arrested, handcuffed, and locked in a cell. The problem, besides the obvious one, was that we had a concert that night we didn't want to miss. And beyond that, we were all minors except for Claydes, who had just turned twenty-one. We weren't released from jail until the next morning, when each of our parents had to come and get us out. We also found out that there had been a riot at the college where we were scheduled to play once they found out we weren't going to make the show.

The drug charges were ridiculous, and we didn't take them seriously because we knew they were bogus. We had a hit song out and a solid record company behind us, so we thought we were untouchable, bulletproof. We saw it as a joke, but the court didn't. The lawyer our manager had recommended told the judge, "These are good boys." Six months later we were still in and out of court, hurrying home for each required court date and then back to our gigs. Finally, the judge said, "The charges are dropped. I don't want to see you guys back here again." To memorialize the episode, we later wrote a song called "Who's Gonna Take the Weight," which became a huge R&B hit.

As we'd discovered, the record business "allegedly" had a lot of organized crime behind it back in the day. "If anybody fucks with youse out on the road, let us know," we were told by a seasoned industry vet. "We'll break their fuckin' legs!" At one point the attorney/manager for the group tried to get us released from our De-Lite contract. He pushed and pushed until he got a phone call from Mr. Wasell in the Bahamas. "I got two words for you: lay off." We later heard that a black Cadillac had pulled up to our manager's driveaway in Montclair, New Jersey, and taken him for a little ride. He was told how he was encroaching on the lion's meal. He called us the next day with a message: "I can't represent or work with you anymore."

At that point the group was basically self-managed for a while. We'd had some modest hits, but we were at a fork in the road after the sales of the most recent album, *Good Times*. We thought it could have done much better than it did. Ronnie and I went to meet Kool and Dennis at High Power Music to talk to Allen Grubman. We started telling him the album was doing well and had plenty of fuel left in the tank. Our live shows continued to help keep the album bouncing around on the charts. He said, "We don't give a fuck how great you are. We don't give a fuck about what geniuses you are or how many instruments you can play. We just want some fucking hits. If you excuse me, gentlemen, I'm on my way to Paris. My wife is waiting for me at the airport."

We left that office and walked down Seventh Avenue bewildered and discouraged. But the more we talked, the more fired up we got. We decided to go straight over to a friend's studio and start experimenting with beats and grooves, mimicking nursery rhymes and spirituals like "Down by the Riverside."

"Can't get enough . . . of that funky stuff," we started singing spontaneously, and it felt right. Then Ricky came in with a bass line that put the song over the edge! Those were the moments I lived for: rehearsal sessions where we all pulled together to create music that represented each of us. We had used that adversity to inform our creative process, and it had worked. It gave us the boost we needed to create two songs, one called "Funky Stuff" and the other "Hollywood Swinging." I could feel the songs were good, and we hoped they would be a hit for our label. We wanted to show that we weren't just a local band with a couple of songs. We were going to be superstars, and these songs were proof.

A few months later, at yet another rehearsal studio, we were working on a song when Ronnie had an idea for a title.

"Why don't we call it 'Jungle Gym'?" he suggested.

Dennis rejected it right away. "No, people are talking a lot about 'boogie.' Let's call it 'Jungle Boogie.'" Everyone quickly agreed.

Don Boyce was "the voice" on that song and became known as the Boogie Man. He was an open, free-spirited person with a deep, booming baritone. Along with his sidekick, Bobby Sims, he introduced me to my first toke of weed and "twisted my arm" to partake of the bounty of female companionship when we were on tour in Germany, even though I was recently married to my high school girlfriend.

The slippery slope lay ahead.

A Lesson in Perseverance

A lot of people think perseverance is easy when you're young and have nothing to lose. That might be true in some respects, but the reality is that perseverance isn't easy for anyone at any age. It takes effort and hard work. The easy way is to give up, to travel the path of least resistance.

The key to perseverance is to understand your motivation and define your goals. I was always crystal clear that I wanted to be a working musician. Music is my God-given talent. It's what I was born to do, and I honored that by following my dream and not giving up.

I defined my goal early on, but I was also careful not to over-define it. I didn't plan on being in a band known around the world, but I welcomed it when it came. I didn't know where the music would lead me, but I knew that if I remained focused and persevered, it would happen as God had intended.

And it did.

2

VERSE

WILD AND PEACEFUL was our fourth studio album, and it launched our band into the musical stratosphere, powered first by introducing the world to "Funky Stuff," which hit number five on the R&B charts and twenty-nine on the pop charts. That song primed the audience for a one-two punch of hits. "Jungle Boogie" set the dance floors and discotheques on fire as it climbed to number two on the R&B charts and number four on the Top 100. The third single unleashed on the eager public was "Hollywood Swinging" in 1974. That jam went to number six on the pop chart, and the album was certified gold.

Making an album is an art, not a science, and we were hyped that we got it right. We were able to make some serious booty-shaking funk infused with the jazz we loved. It was amazing to watch the faces in the audience when those funky grooves washed over them in a live setting. We got a thrill out of watching them sing all the words to the songs we'd worked so hard to perfect.

That album was our hot, sexy, musical calling card as we announced to the world that Kool & the Gang was a band to be taken seriously. We might have been young—I had just turned twenty-five when

"Hollywood Swinging" came out—but we had been playing for years at that point. We were the real deal: true musicians who were able to deliver the goods while staying true to our roots. Ricky handled a lot of the vocals while Kool delivered on the bass, Claydes strummed the guitar, and I held the beat that centered us as our musical star soared into orbit.

We were finally garnering national attention as the *New York Times* heralded us "a breath of fresh air," and we booked gigs on national TV shows. We had been playing gigs all over the country to support the album and took any opportunity to get more exposure.

We played on a weekly show called *In Concert*, a Dick Clark production that aired late on Friday nights as a showcase for the hottest new acts. It was a time before music videos were popular, so shows like that and *Midnight Special* were ways for artists to connect with audiences all over the country. We played that show twice. The first time was in March 1974, on the same show as rockers Foghat and Kiss. We were asked back in January 1975, along with Bobby Vinton and Earth, Wind & Fire. Other artists who played that show included Chuck Berry, Bo Diddley, Sly and the Family Stone, B.B. King, Gladys Knight, Miles Davis, and Al Green. It was an amazing music venue.

On June 1, 1974, we were booked on the most influential and longest-running music program of the time, *Soul Train*, for the first of many appearances. The show aired in syndication and played on most outlets on the weekend, when everyone was home and glued to their TV for a weekly dose of soul and R&B, not to mention the amazing hosting duties of music impresario Don Cornelius. Of course I'd watched many episodes of the show. I got excited every week as that train of funk chugged across the railroad tracks of the country, delivering musical goodness along the way in the animated opening. I loved the dance party atmosphere and the performers who graced the stage each week.

By that time our live act was tight, and on our first appearance, we chose to wear matching suits of varying colors. I was perched in the back and keeping time on the drums in my blue threads as we opened with "Funky Stuff." The party people seemed to love it when those horns kicked off the song, not to mention the trademark whistle we used long before songs like "Bad Girls" joined the trend.

We came back later in the show and had changed up our outfits by switching the jackets to give a different vibe. We launched into "Jungle Boogie," and as the band sang the harmonies, Don Boyce bellowed out the almost spoken-word lyrics. He rocked the stage as the only member wearing a hat, which he tipped ever so slightly as he grooved his way through the song. We also played our first number-one R&B single, "Hollywood Swinging," the song that Nile Rodgers said he based the Chic hit "Good Times" on. (Much later, the song even appeared on the hit video game *Grand Theft Auto: San Andreas*.)

As George "Funky" Brown, I was still acclimating to the celebrity lifestyle and the groupies who came with it. There were countless crazy incidents, like a girl who leaped into our limo and pulled a screwdriver on Gene Redd when he told her to get out. If I'd been around that many women a few years earlier, things might have been different, but I was already married.

We met at seventeen and fell in love. We were married in 1970, when I was twenty-one. At that time she was in college, and I was a struggling musician. We had two children together, but the cracks in our relationship were already threatening the stability of our foundation. One problem—and it was a big one—was that as my career progressed, her interest waned. That was difficult to accept, because it was a huge part of my life, and it was the part that she didn't want to even hear about. It was the classic story of two people marrying young and growing apart as they grew up. When my career took off, it only served to create more distance between us, not just physically but emotionally.

Every aspect of my life was changing, and I could see that with success came plenty of challenges—things I'd never expected. For example, I was afraid to tell my mother that I was moving out of the house to a high-rise uptown apartment, doorman and all. It felt like I was leaving my family and friends behind because I could afford a different lifestyle. It was clear that with the hit record and the money flowing, my life would never be the same.

One thing that didn't change among the group was our faith. In fact, it grew deeper as we experienced other cultures. On our first European tour, Ronald was given a Koran. He read it cover to cover on the tour bus in Germany. Kool read *Message to the Blackman in America* by Elijah Muhammad. I read another of his books, *How to Eat to Live*. Several members made a religious conversion and even changed names: Ronald to Ronald Five X and Kool to Robert Nine X. The family name was changed from Bell to Bayyan ("clear evidence"), as the old one was considered a slave name. Ronald soon changed his name again, this time to Khalis. The rest of the band was given an ultimatum: convert or you're out.

I felt at first that they had become overzealous, getting too preachy from the stage ("the White man is the devil"), which alienated a lot of the concertgoers, both Black and White. Don't get me wrong, religion is an important, enriching part of life, but I did not think we had to hit people over the head with the guilt stick of faith. We had learned that music by itself could touch people divinely. It was perhaps no coincidence that the band got its start jamming at churches, first at the Incarnation and then at the Ankh. Maybe Father Avery and Father Castle saw the potential in us before we did. Praise be to God!

The stress and tension that come along with success can make people engage in destructive acts: drinking, smoking, overeating, taking drugs, screwing a lot, and going totally out of your mind. I worked hard not to succumb to the pressure, although it was difficult under the circumstances. We had just experienced our first big hit, and

I was not so keen to jump off. I was determined to keep a healthy perspective regarding the Nation of Islam movement and the controversies surrounding it. I was able to take everything with a grain of salt and focus on things that were important to me. I learned a lot about dietary laws and keeping the body fit, and with a healthy body, I was able to stay grounded and remember that all paths lead to God. As we got deeper into the '70s, our fame and wealth exploded. The vices that I *did* develop were smoking cigarettes, smoking weed, and drinking cognac. Fortunately, I never got pulled down into the swirling depths of hard drugs.

Next on our musical journey was the release of "Spirit of the Boogie," which was put out on a 45. Then we got word that in Chicago, a radio DJ had flipped it over and played the B-side, which was "Summer Madness," and "the phones lit up," as they used to say. So after the first song reached number one on the R&B charts and began to slide, the instrumental "Summer Madness" took over and went to number thirty-five on the Hot 100. It became one of the most sampled R&B songs ever, used in the *Rocky* movie in 1976, a video game, and a shoe commercial.

By the late '70s we were making a few TV appearances, playing gigs, and getting in the recording studio as much as we could, when out of nowhere, the demand we'd had in the past began to fade. It was the height of the disco era, and in music, trends come and go. If you don't jump on board, you can get left behind. We'd always been a party band, so we were willing to give the new craze a try. We put out the album *Open Sesame* in 1976, and the title track was a hit, reaching number six on the R&B chart. Another song, "Super Band," rose to number seventeen.

In November 1977 the movie *Saturday Night Fever* debuted and was an instant smash, depicting the life of a young man enmeshed in the disco dance craze that had taken over not only the radio airwaves but the entire country. The movie only helped to elevate the status of disco music in popular culture. The film brought in almost $26 million in the first month and has earned more than $237 million worldwide. A true smash! A crucial part of that movie was the dancing scenes and, of course, the music. By a stroke of luck, "Open Sesame" was chosen for the film and included on the soundtrack, unlike "Spirit of the Boogie" in the *Rocky* movie.

The song played an integral role in one of the dance-off scenes set at a local discotheque. The bumping tune, with its funk-infused groove punctuated with shouts of "Open Sesame!" and "Abracadabra!" gave the movie and the soundtrack some much-needed street cred. Fortunately, being on the *Saturday Night Fever* soundtrack was a huge opportunity for us because that album became number one around the world, won a Grammy, and became one of the top-selling albums of all time, surpassing forty million copies.

Encouraged by the success of that soundtrack and practically any song with a disco beat, we tossed our musical hat into the ring with our next two albums, *The Force* and *Everybody's Dancin'*. The albums performed unevenly, with the first going only to number 142 on the *Billboard* charts and the second not charting at all. We'd tried our hand at our version of disco by giving it a dash of musical flavor that we thought would be embraced by our old fans and reach new fans. It didn't work.

Our early success and the boost from *Saturday Night Fever* were amazing, but success doesn't prepare you for the decline that invariably happens. We were just hitting our stride, finding our groove with each other and our audience, when things went left. It was discouraging to put so much hard work into music that did not live up to our expectations. I knew we hadn't yet reached our creative peak, and there was no logical reason we should have been in that position.

We had the musical chops to go much further, yet our career idled and then stalled completely. Even the music shows on TV weren't calling us anymore. During that time we had a few appearances on

shows like *Soul Alive, Horas Doradas,* and *The Mike Douglas Show,*
and that was over a three-year period. At least it kept us in the public
eye while we crafted our next career move.

On a personal level, I could feel the change within my family and
friends. It was unnerving, because I was the same person I was before
the success, but with our star dimming and the flow of money slowing,
we were all unsure how to navigate the situation. No one gives you
the tools to deal with such a highly public career decline. There's no
handbook to help figure it out. I could feel the energy shift when I
walked into a room, the disappointment behind the supportive smiles
and encouraging words. I could imagine what they were thinking. *Is
the ride over? Did Kool & the Gang go as far as they could go?*

I was going through a professional downturn that had an impact
on me personally and financially. At one point I had exhausted all the
money in my account. To make matters worse, there was trouble at
home. Early in our marriage, my profession was exciting, a world of
unlimited opportunity, an experience my wife and I shared. However,
as the demands on my time increased, my support system became
the band and our management. There was little for her to do but
watch from the sidelines. She had her own dreams and, as a result,
the chasm between us became irreparable.

We made the decision to divorce while our two young boys were
enrolled at the Bergen School in New Jersey. It was a small school
with a controlled attendance of around a hundred students. I would
do everything I could to keep them in a good school that would help
prepare them for a good future, especially as young Black men. That
was very important to me and their mother.

So I decided to get back to my musical roots by attending school
to study the dramatic arts for six months. I had a little bit of money
but needed more. With nowhere else to turn, I approached my mother
and my stepfather, who was a policeman. It was humbling to be in
that situation after having achieved an enviable level of success, been

on TV, and performed around the country, but they agreed to give me the $2,000 I needed.

However, I still had other bills, so I paid a visit to the Jamaican gentleman who managed the band to see if I could get an advance. As I walked along Fifty-Seventh Street toward Gramercy Park, I looked around at the people passing on the sidewalk. I focused on each of them and their mannerisms and styles, and especially on how they moved. In my mind I associated their gait with a jazz bass line: *Do do do do, do do da do.*

I nixed the visit to our manager's office and hurried back home to sit down at the piano. I settled on a C-minor chord that changed to a seventh chord. Then I chose an F7 chord, and it flowed naturally into G, B-flat, C, E, F, and C-minor 7 to a C-minor chord, then back to the F straight up. Next I changed keys, a signature Funky George move.

It was obvious to me that I had the beginnings of a hit on my hands.

Get Down Tonight

There is no denying that when it rains, it pours. My personal life seemed to be on the same trajectory as my professional success. It was difficult navigating the divorce while trying to emerge from a creative funk to come up with hit music that just might revive our career.

As a spiritual guy, I've always placed my belief in myself and ultimately God to see me through the hard times. I can't say that being a musician was the cause for the breakup of my marriage, but it certainly didn't help. If I'd been an accountant or had an office job, maybe things would have been different. There's no denying that it takes a certain type of person to handle a spouse in the entertainment industry. It's a world of magic and make-believe, and at times it can get difficult to tell what's real and what isn't. But it's the only life I've ever known.

Around 1979 the band experienced two changes that altered our musical journey and paved the way for our domination of the charts for the next ten years. First the band decided to bring on a dedicated lead singer instead of trading off vocals to fit a song. A singer would put a face to the band and give us some vocal consistency that the audience could relate to. I was excited about the change, and I'd seen how well our peers had done with a similar lineup: a strong band with a commanding lead singer. There were the Commodores with Lionel Richie, Earth, Wind & Fire with Maurice White and Philip Bailey, and the Trammps with Jimmy Ellis, to name just a few.

James Taylor was a teacher in New Jersey and an aspiring singer who played nightclubs and eventually joined a band called Full Force. We needed a singer, and he came to the House of Music studio to see if he would be a good fit for the band. It had to be an intimidating experience for him, because the music studio is a hallowed space, a safe zone for creativity, a place where missteps can lead to musical magic. But it takes time for a band to achieve that level of creative comfort and freedom. Outsiders either sink or swim. They must integrate quickly, intuitively, and instinctively, or it won't work. Bringing on James "J.T." Taylor, the only singer we auditioned, as our vocalist was followed quickly by probably the most strategic professional move we could have made. We needed a new producer to help guide us. Our first choice was Stevie Wonder. We contacted him, and he showed interest but was already committed to other projects. It all worked out for the best, because we teamed up with famed music producer Eumir Deodato. He was from Brazil and had won a Grammy in 1974 for Best Pop Instrumental for a song called "Also Sprach Zarathustra (2001)."

I think he was such a talented producer because he was also an incredibly accomplished musician. Beginning in 1964, he had played on, arranged, and produced many songs. He was quite talented and, as we soon found out, so easy to work with. He knew how to get the best out of us as a band, and he was also skilled at making hits, the holy grail for every record company. With J.T. on board, we were ready to take on the world. Having a voice and a presence to write for helped me tailor songs to J.T.'s strengths, and he was a songwriter as well and understood what worked for him. It was at that point that we reached musical nirvana, the perfect trifecta of a seasoned band, a gifted producer, and a talented singer.

I was living in Gramercy Park at the time, and all the guys would come to my apartment to hang out. We goofed off in the park, tossed around a Frisbee, and, of course, jammed and worked on songs when we felt inspired. So when I had the idea for a song, I'd already come up with the melody and chord changes. One day when we were all in the studio jamming and experimenting as usual, I went to J.T. and played what I'd written, because I wanted to get his input as the vocalist. "Hey, man, I like this," he said quickly. Khalis mentioned something about ladies' night, a popular promotion at nightclubs to bring in women. We often went to clubs like Studio 54, where it was ladies' night every Friday.

That phrase was added to the groove I had created along with some of my lyrics about living on Fifty-Seventh Street with no money. I think it was J.T. who mentioned adding "disco lights," and it continued from there. We continued to build on the music along with the lyrics, and "Ladies' Night" was born.

Those lyrics came from my experience walking down the streets of Manhattan, usually heading to our manager's office to ask for money, because I was dealing with my kids and the divorce. Despite feeling down, I couldn't help coming up with a bass line while watching folks parade up and down the street. When it was time to put it all together, I sat down at the piano and instantly had an anxiety attack. That was how powerful the music was inside of me. It would consume me—still does. I'd feel the music so intensely that I'd be temporarily unable to continue. It was like the musical dreams I had as a child. Putting poetry to music always came naturally to me. I could picture how the lyrics, music, and harmonies could fit together just right. It wasn't something I could ignore.

So I took a moment to relax and allow myself to calm down. Once I was ready, I sat at the piano and began to play. "*Señor*," Eumir said, "that's exactly what we've been looking for!" He reacted just as enthusiastically as J.T. had earlier. Encouraged, I sang some of the lyrics as Khalis joined in. I manipulated the keys a bit, we added our trademark horns, and it turned into a dance song. I could tell when it was all coming together like that—I just knew it was right. I loved those times when everything clicked, and the band jumped in instinctively to guide the song to completion.

Collaborating was always magical between us. Maybe it's because we had known each other since we were kids, but we always had a way of coming together for the music, regardless of any other nonsense that was going on. Khalis used to call it "the collective genius of Kool & the Gang," and I think he had a point. Khalis, Ricky, Spike, Charles, and I wrote much of the material that might also be massaged by other writers on our team. Using that process helped us find the best songs possible, because so many of us participated. We put all our ideas together to come up with the music that represented the Kool & the Gang sound.

One day J.T. and his girlfriend at the time came into the recording studio while I was playing the baby grand. Knowing that J.T. wouldn't bring in anyone who didn't respect our space, I continued with my musical experimentation.

She said, "George, what are you doing?"

I smiled and said, "Making a bunch of mistakes, you know?"

She screwed up her face. "Great things come out of mistakes."

That got me thinking. She was right about that. The song didn't have to be perfect, it just had to continually evolve until it was ready. It got me thinking about the struggles I'd been through at such a young age—falling in love at seventeen, getting married, going through a divorce, weathering career ups and downs. It was a lot for a young guy, and it informed my songwriting. Sometimes, I wanted to run for shelter, hide away until things were better, but life doesn't work that way.

I wrote all the lyrics to a song called "Too Hot" on a paper bag I found in a lobby. I'd already played a rough version of the song for our previous manager. He didn't like it and said it sounded too much like a Stevie Wonder tune. (I didn't see that as a bad thing!)

It was a change in direction—we had done songs like "Summer Madness," but we didn't really focus on ballads, even mid-tempo ones. I was still determined to have the group record it, and I even offered "splits" so we could divide any profits from it. No one took me up on that. So I walked home feeling somewhat dejected. Still, maybe to appease me, it was released along with "Ladies' Night" and *bingo*! It was a hit!

We eventually divided the royalties of the hit song "Too Hot," because that was best for the group dynamic. Arguing over percentages wouldn't serve any of us, but I did learn early on how important songwriting credits and royalty percentages are to a musician's livelihood and legacy.

"Ladies' Night" was released as an album and a single. It went on to reach number eight on the Hot 100 and lives on in infamy. It was released on an album with the same title and as a single with "Too Hot" on the B-side. Those were two of the first songs that Eumir produced and J.T. sang lead on, so that showed us that we had made the right decision in bringing those two talents on board.

That atmosphere of musical freedom, of give and take, turned out to be a perfect place for me to shine. As a musician and a lyricist, I could hear in a song what many others couldn't. For example, on the song "Take My Heart (You Can Have It If You Want It)," Claydes Smith wrote the track in 12/8 time, meaning that the quarter notes had three eighth notes with four beats times three sub-beats to equal

12/8. It was a different tempo from most of our songs. Some of the guys said they didn't like the track. So I took the song home and worked on it with a female singer who agreed to help us out. As I wrote, she sang the parts for me until I looked down and realized we had a complete song. I brought it to J.T., and he said, "Hey, man, this is good stuff!"

Eumir continued to bring even more structure to our group and helped facilitate our natural collaborative process. He would give us a time to show up to the studio, and sometimes he'd even swing by my place in Gramercy Park to pick me up. That way he could make sure the band showed up when we were supposed to.

He'd say, "Good morning, George. Let me see your homework."

I'd pull out my yellow legal pad and either hum the tune or sing the lyrics and wait for his reaction. If he wasn't feeling it, he'd yawn and say, "Aww, that's so cute." But if he liked it, there was no doubt about it. "Yes, that's what we need, *señor*! Let's keep working on this!"

Our typical work hours at the studio were 11 AM to 8 PM. That schedule suited us, because most musicians are by nature not morning people, and it left us time in the evening to have somewhat of a social life. Then we could go home and do our homework and get up to do it all again the next day. Eumir held us accountable, and that yielded results, because we all wanted the same thing: great music for the fans.

He helped us take the R&B/funk sound that we were known for and tailor it to the pop market. That combination built our longevity, because we were no longer pegged in one genre. We could go from jazz to R&B and now to pop. Eumir was such a musician's musician that he really helped us reach our full potential. So with him on board and J.T. ready to show out on vocals, it was musical serendipity.

I'd always enjoyed playing not only the drums but piano as well. One day I told Eumir that I'd like to take classical piano lessons to broaden my abilities and hone my talent.

"No, no, don't do that," he said. "You'll mess up what you already have!"

I did it anyway, because I didn't want to be the unskilled guy. I wanted to refine my craft and see if there were other techniques I could learn and improve upon. (To be honest, I'm still studying to this day.)

Eumir could remember phrasing or a snippet from the horn section that someone had played days prior. He'd say, "Remember what you did that time with the horns? Let's try that here, but be careful with the melodies. No more than three melodies; otherwise, the listener gets confused. Also, be mindful of the runs, because they can go in and out of tune if we're not careful." He was focused on maintaining vocal control and honoring the melody.

That's not to say it was always peaches and cream. Just like every band, things could get messy, and egos could take over. It's natural in that kind of environment and under that kind of pressure to prove yourself as a musician and as a band. The stakes are high, and a lot of money and lives were dependent on how successful a song or album was.

At one point Kool, Khalis, and I secured a meeting with the influential Clive Davis at Arista Records. Fueled by youthful bravado, we were sure that he would be enamored of our big ideas. We stood around his desk, and he said, "I know you guys are hitmakers, but I have to hear something. What do you have?"

"Well, we've got ideas, Clive," one of us said. "Lots of ideas!"

He responded, "Everyone's got ideas. I need to hear something." We left feeling somewhat dejected, but a few months later, we were performing at the American Music Awards, and he was in the front row sitting beside Whitney Houston. It was a good feeling when he congratulated us along with Whitney, Michael Jackson, and a host of other music legends.

When the Jacksons had a compound in Encino, I used to go there to work on recordings and song production. Later on, when I had my own home studio, Jermaine would come by to hang out or work on some stuff. Kool & the Gang has also toured with the Jacksons, so we all have history and camaraderie that has lasted for many years.

Once "Ladies' Night" was an undeniable hit and a multiplatinum record, we were playing at the Lincoln Center, and my mom and stepdad were there to see us. After the show I gave Mom $10,000 to cover the $2,000 they had lent me during those lean times, plus a little interest. She used that money to buy a house near Lincoln Park in Jersey City. It was a huge house, maybe fifteen thousand square feet, and it overlooked the park. She hosted large family gatherings for every holiday and special occasion.

We were flying high with the success of "Ladies' Night" and "Too Hot," but we had no idea another song was about to launch us into the pop-culture stratosphere.

Leave the Cuckoo in the Clock

Touring to support an album has always been an obligation of any serious band, and Kool & the Gang was no exception. Thinking back on those days, I remember being involved in plenty of rock 'n' roll mischief—"malfunctions" as my mother would say—and other hijinks, such as turning over furniture in hotels or trashing dressing rooms. I was far tamer than most. I never really broke anything, didn't cause any significant damage. But the fact that it was de rigueur for musicians made it an acceptable form of self-expression. It was a therapeutic way of letting off steam, but I never took it to an extreme.

We had a couple of experienced road managers named Charlie and Sam who worked together to handle our band and the logistics of touring. Charlie had called Sam, who was working with Stevie Wonder, and asked him to join our tour. Sam was the definition of "old school." Back in the day, he went on the road with all the heavyweight jazz musicians. In fact, he learned how to manage bands by working for a well-known jazz promoter named George Wein.

When we'd get into some mischief, Sam would just shake his head and say, "Mmm, mmm, mmm, you boys . . ." If there were women involved, he'd say, "Keep those bitches off the wings of the stage or just leave them alone. They're all up to no good. Leave those bitches at home." He may have been somewhat coarse, but I understood his intent. Problems were inevitable on the road, and the more relationships involved, the more complicated things became.

Sam knew what he was talking about, because he'd originally started as a baseball player at a time when Blacks were just beginning to join the league. The gossip was that he'd gotten involved with a White girl and things didn't turn out well. The incident apparently shut down his chances to play ball. There's no denying the guy had challenges in his relationships, and he regaled us with salacious stories as we traveled from one city to the next.

Looking back on those days, our actions were quite innocent. We played touch football in the five-star hotel hallways, since our floors were off limits to anyone outside of the band. We used to have water gun battles in the hotel stairwells, rarely anything intentionally destructive or malicious. It was more of a bonding experience and a time to get out a little pent-up energy or any ill feelings among group members.

Today when we tour, things are much different, because we are in different stages of our lives. There is no more importing girlfriends from different cities, states, or countries. No more limo rides up to 145th Street to the Jamaican health food store for weed. No more rationing the Valium, Xanax, or other "little helpers." No more girls asking me to get them pregnant, as they did while I was married with one child and another on the way. It's not shocking, I suppose, but some don't realize how different life is on the road. Reality blurs and fantasy takes over—if you let it.

Back then we usually doubled up in hotel rooms, and I often bunked with Charlie. He played blues piano and had a daughter, Tyler Collins, who had a hit record with the song "Girls Nite Out." She was also in several movies, including Bill Duke's *A Rage in Harlem*. (She has a great voice, and recently we have worked on projects together.)

Charlie and I became very good friends and remain so to this very day. Sam, God bless him, passed away in 2014. Upon his death he took with him countless stories of debauchery and mayhem that are probably best left to the imagination.

I'll Never Do That Again . . . Until I Do

When we started out in the '70s, the fans went crazy. We were very young, and to see all of those teenage girls screaming at the stage was exciting but overwhelming. After the show they tried to hop in our limos, but as we tried to pull away, it was just total madness. Sometimes, we had to stay inside the theater for hours after the show and wait for the crowd to dissipate, but those fans were relentless.

Some would just wait and wait and wait. In the '80s the frenzy only increased, with female fans surrounding our cars and jumping on the hoods. Occasionally it went on for so long that it was like we'd entered a parallel universe, watching ourselves trapped in our cars unable to leave the venue. The novelty wore off quickly for me, once I realized it could last for hours if someone didn't intervene. It's not that I didn't like the attention, but I was a drummer who just wanted to focus on the music. Well, most of the time anyway.

International travel was exciting at first as well, especially our trips to Africa. I had no idea what to expect from fans in a different country, and it was even more chaotic than in the States. I would look out over a sea of people, a swelling mass of indistinguishable faces bobbing up and down as the crowd shifted and swayed. We were often unable to get through the crowd to reach the venue. Like in the United States, they circled our cars, and we were hostages once again.

Seeing that obsession and pandemonium up close was a sobering experience. Of course, as a musician the fantasy was to have women throwing themselves at you, but being in the middle of that estrogen storm was not as I'd anticipated. The glazed look in their eyes, the steely focus, the determination. It was just unreal. When we were finally able to get back to the hotel after the show, the lobby was always full of women just waiting for a glimpse of the band—and more if they had it their way.

When I ordered room service, the female employees sometimes lingered in the room to ask things like "How does it feel to be a star?" It was flattering, but all I could think about was the food. If they wouldn't take the hint, I'd say I didn't feel well and needed to be alone. I didn't want to hurt their feelings, and in the beginning, I was worried about upsetting any of the fans we had worked so hard to cultivate. I didn't want to give the band a reputation for being rude and unfriendly. It wasn't until later that I realized I had to do what was right for me and my well-being, even though they were usually hoping to be asked to stay for a while. It's not as if I never did that, but there was a time and place.

Sometimes, I got a call from the front desk.

"Hey, my name is Candy. What are you doing now?"

"Uh, I'm lying in the bed?"

"Can I come up on my break?"

As we traveled around the country as the headline band, many times we met up with other touring acts trying to build their following. If we were all in the same vicinity, that meant endless parties, usually late into the night to keep the adrenaline rush from the performance alive for as long as possible. One time we met up with the Bar-Kays ("Hit and Run") and had the run of an entire hotel floor. Needless to say, young ladies paraded by throughout the night.

Sometimes, we even jumped on the bus of other bands if they were going in the same direction. I'd ride with the Gap Band ("You Dropped a Bomb on Me") and talk about how crazy things had gotten the night before and what was to come at the next gig. At the hotel, girls fluttered toward us like moths to a flame.

The ladies could be shy and flirty, or there was the flip side. Many times women told me straight out, "Please knock me up. Please. I just want to have your baby." Other times, I'd invite a young lady to my room, and by the time I closed the door and turned around, she was on the bed, stark naked and ready for some fun.

Sometimes, a woman invited me to her place, since she lived nearby. It was a nice change from the chaos and occasional orgies that occurred at the hotels with so many sexually charged young people in one location. I spent the night at one lady's house, and in the morning I was in the living room when a little boy ran by giggling! I had no idea anyone else was home. Come to find out, her husband was a private pilot for a famous athlete, and he was often gone for weeks at a time.

I still had vices back then: smoking and drinking cognac. I learned quickly that if I let alcohol control my actions, I could very well find myself in even worse situations. Yet those ladies could be quite clever and calculating. It reminded me of the Motown song "The Hunter Gets Captured by the Game," by the Marvelettes. It was written by Smokey Robinson and told the story from a woman's point of view. It was about setting "a tender trap" by stalking a man to learn about his habits so she could catch him.

As I became a seasoned musician traveling the world, I saw the same patterns of obsession and calculation. It didn't matter where we were, that cat-and-mouse game of seeking pleasure while protecting yourself was universal. There was sometimes a slight difference because of the culture, but the result was the same: the exhilaration of sleeping with a man who was on TV and the radio playing addictive hit songs.

There were times—more than I can count—that I realized afterward that I'd fallen into the familiar pattern that I'd sworn to avoid. There's something about the monotony of travel that messes with your mind. Being on stage for two hours is nirvana. That's what fuels me to get out there, because for me there is nothing better than playing music for an appreciative audience. It's the incredible amount of time offstage that breeds temptation to relieve the unavoidable boredom.

Sometimes, I wonder exactly how many thousands of miles we traveled on those raggedy buses in the early years. Back then, those buses were incredibly uncomfortable, from the rigid, upright seats to the windows that didn't latch properly. That's not even considering the invariably worn-out shock absorbers. We felt every bump and pothole as the bus ambled its way to the next concert, often on narrow side roads to avoid traffic and reach the venue on time.

We would remove several rows of seats to make room for our instruments and travel bags, using a rope to tether them in place. Sometimes, we'd lay on the nearby seats and use our feet to steady the gear so it wouldn't fall over as we barreled down the road.

As our success grew, we got to upgrade our mode of transportation. It wasn't long before we were able to purchase our own bus, an old Greyhound double-decker! We were movin' on up, like George and Weezy! It felt like we'd hit the big time. We even had our own driver, a man named Harry who was a real slick cat. He'd been in the music scene for years and was good friends with Marvin Gaye.

He drove us all around the South, usually straight through the night. We could be on that bus for eighteen hours straight, because we had to make the next gig on time; otherwise, our reputation could be impacted. Word travels fast among promoters and music venues.

Often, when it was maybe two or three o'clock in the morning, Harry would go, "Oh, Lord." We'd be out cold, and he'd grab the microphone of the PA system and say, "Hey Kool, you awake?" We'd all jump up in our seats, our intermittent napping interrupted by the squelching feedback from the speakers. "Hey Kool, Kool. You know Blind Lemon Jefferson, the blues artist?"

"What?"

"He was part of the Five Blind Boys. I know you remember the Five Blind Boys."

"It's two o'clock in the morning, Harry. You're yelling over the speaker system in the bus."

"OK, let me tell you about those cats."

Harry was a real character and always trying to fix me up with "a nice girl." He'd poke my shoulder and say, "George, how's it going with that young lady you were seeing in Brooklyn? You still see her?"

As the band's popularity grew, we sometimes traveled separately. Once, while most of the band traveled by bus, I got in a car to go to the airport and fly to Indiana for a gig. My driver turned on the car radio, and we heard that Kool & the Gang had been involved in a bus accident because, apparently, the driver had fallen asleep. It was scary, but it turned out that no one suffered injuries and the show went on as scheduled.

When traveling internationally, the journey was often unpredictable. We were going to Germany, and I boarded a 747 out of Newark. We were taxiing down when the plane engine started to make a groaning noise. We took off and flew over the Atlantic Ocean, and suddenly there was an explosion. The left engine had gone, and the plane began to list to one side. Fortunately, the skilled pilot knew what to do. He emptied the fuel onboard and landed back in Newark. (Apparently, he couldn't land with a plane full of fuel.)

We were fortunate that it happened before we got some altitude, because it could have been disastrous. All the passengers boarded the next available plane, but I declined. I said, "I'll stay at this hotel tonight and sort it out in the morning." I knew from my grandmother not to tempt fate. It was best to take a beat and start fresh the next day.

Once, I was flying over Alaska when the captain came on the intercom and said, "Ladies and gentlemen, we don't have enough fuel. We just don't have enough fuel, and we're going to have to land at an alternative airport." We were flying over a frozen tundra in Alaska, and apparently we were running dangerously low.

Then we were on a flight to South Carolina, and once again we got to North Carolina and the pilot said we were low on fuel. He had to land at an alternate airport.

The first time we flew on a private jet, we were headed to Rochester to perform on a bill with the incomparable Nina Simone. It was raining and then snowing as we flew through the choppy winter sky. The next thing I knew, the wings were icing up. Claydes just laughed it off, because he was fearless. Then the pilot said, "Let's see if our tax dollars are working," as he radioed the tower. I found that the pilots are much more direct on a private plane. No sugarcoating things. "There's too much rain, and we can't turn around," he told us.

Apparently, there was an issue with the weight distribution, which is much more crucial on a smaller plane. On that trip we had so many people and so much luggage that we had to stack the bags against the cockpit door. The pilot couldn't have gotten out if he needed to. We were all squeezed in like sardines.

Much later in our career, we found ourselves flying to Egypt in two Gulfstreams, one for the crew and another for the band. We zipped right over the pyramids, and the pilot tilted the plane so we could get a better look.

That was a wild ride.

A Lesson in Patience

The constant travel can mess with your head in ways you never imagined. I always saw myself as someone intuitive and able to read people and their motives. Sometimes, that went right out the window in a touring situation, especially as our popularity grew.

I had female personal assistants whom I vetted and hired once I was satisfied with their intentions, only to find that they were aspiring singers or actresses. Their goal was always to get closer to the action, to find a way into the notoriously impenetrable industry. Some wanted to be with me for little more than bragging rights.

People ask my current wife, "What does it feel like being with a star?"

"He's like any other guy," she responds.

It's like the story John Lennon often told. He was notoriously approachable after leaving the Beatles, and one time a man came up to him in London and shared his love of John's work. John graciously invited him inside his home for some breakfast. The man told John, "I follow everything you do. I read everything about you. It's like your work is speaking to me. I feel such a connection to you."

John responded, "I'm just writing for Yoko."

Practically any time an artist creates a song or other type of work that resonates with many people, it's something that comes from personal experience. A skillful songwriter can craft the words so they resonate with the listeners; they can relate to the universal sentiments. Others see in the work what they want to see. They connect it to their own experiences, adjust the narrative to fit their lives, their situations. That gives them a sense of commonality with the artist that naturally evokes more emotions, even to the point of fantasy.

Most people don't realize that much of that art comes from a place of frustration or even rage. The creative process is rarely fueled by peace and happiness. It evolves from difficulty and strife. The magic is being able to channel that emotion into something beautiful and universal.

When I'm creating, I'm never making choices so that it will be a hit song. Of course I hope it will be, and often I can feel when it's likely to happen, but there are no guarantees. Musicians want their work to reach and impact as many people as possible. That's our goal, but the focus is on the beauty of the song. What feeling does it evoke? What imagery is conveyed?

For me those early experiences with travel and the excess of fame taught me to exercise patience amid the chaos that often ensued. I learned that I couldn't control what was happening around me, whether it was bad weather, a beat-up Greyhound bus, or a plane with mechanical issues.

It's important to remember the power of patience in our lives, whether it's in our jobs, our relationships, or our personal goals. We often want instant gratification, but as a working musician who has played everywhere from dingy clubs to massive stadiums, success is about putting in the work, focusing on your goals, and never giving up. And that's easy to do if you truly enjoy the journey.

Patience allows us to navigate life's challenges more effectively without getting unnecessarily frustrated. That's important, because it helps us build better relationships. It's the difference between one-night stands and a lasting connection. Patience is also key to good mental and physical health.

In my journey through life, I've learned that patience can become a reality by making a conscious effort to think things through instead of responding with pure, unfiltered emotions. Practicing mindfulness can also help bring clarity to a situation by simply taking a step back, breathing deeply, and taking stock of your situation.

Finally, I've learned that feeling grateful for even small accomplishments makes reaching those bigger goals even more rewarding.

3

PRE-CHORUS

B Y 1980 WE HAD ALREADY PUT OUT ELEVEN STUDIO ALBUMS, and that's not count-ing the live records. There's no denying that we were a hardworking band from the jump. We were focused on creating music and taking over the charts. With the phenomenal success of "Ladies' Night" and "Too Hot," we were on a creative streak and had officially recovered from the slump of the late '70s. The success felt amazing and grew our audience to an even broader swath of the population thanks to the infusion of R&B and pop.

In 1980, while we were traveling in a bus, Ronald (Khalis) had the idea for an anthem song. It was inspired by a few key lyrics from "Ladies' Night" combined with religious teachings from the Koran and references to celebrating when God created Adam. The collective genius of Kool & the Gang was once again on full display as we helped guide the song to completion. The tune was an instant hit with the help of J.T.'s vocals and the tempo of 123 beats per minute. Khalis accomplished his goal of creating not only an anthem but a worldwide phenomenon that is still played at countless weddings, birthdays, and other celebrations all around the world. It was called "Celebration."

The song climbed to the top spot on the Billboard Hot 100 and also reached number one on the R&B and dance charts. It was clearly a hit across the board. Something we could never have anticipated was that it would be played as a celebration of the U.S. hostages being released from Iran in 1981. In 2021 the song was added to the National Recording Registry at the Library of Congress for being "culturally, historically, or aesthetically significant."

Celebrate

We dutifully stuck to our goal of putting out an album a year, and 1981 yielded *Something Special*. Riding high on the popularity of "Celebration," we had more hits on our hands with songs like "Steppin' Out," "Take My Heart," and of course "Get Down on It," which climbed the charts and was certified gold.

As One came out in 1982, but it was not as successful as the others. The singles "Let's Go Dancin'" and "Big Fun" did well, but that was the extent of it. It was difficult to see that we were losing the momentum of our previous two albums, but in the music business, there are no guarantees. Musical tastes were changing, as they always do. Disco was morphing into more of a pop/dance vibe, and R&B was evolving as well.

Industry heavyweights work tirelessly to predict the next trend and monitor musical tastes to give the audience what they want, but we learned that was a recipe for failure, at least for us. All we wanted to do was make great music that made us feel good and hopefully resonated with the audience. It was a balancing act of appealing to new fans while still giving our faithful audience what they had come to expect from Kool & the Gang.

Unfortunately, it was clear that *As One* wasn't going to perform as we'd hoped. That ended up being the last album Eumir produced for the group. He'd done an amazing job working with the band, and his influence was undeniable. He was able to give us structure and guide our creative energies into great music. However, the decision was made, and he had many other projects to focus on.

In 1983 we released *In the Heart*, with the band acting as its own producer alongside a man named Jim Bonnefond. Thanks to the pop ballad "Joanna," led by the creativity of Claydes and J.T., the album was a hit, and we were back on top. "Joanna" rose to number two on the charts and was followed by the singles "Tonight" and "Straight Ahead."

The next year, we were working at a popular recording studio in the Bahamas for a couple of months, putting together what would be the *Emergency* album. It was an amazing time in a studio filled with energy and excitement. Musically, we were firing on all cylinders. Then we got a call from Elton John's team. He was on his Breaking Hearts tour, with plans to play over sixty shows in North America, but first he was producing an epic show that would take place at Wembley Stadium. It was called the Night and Day concert, because it included an afternoon show and then another at night to be broadcast on BBC Radio 1. Other artists on the bill were Big Country, Wang Chung, and Nik Kershaw. It was to be the last of his world tours for a while, so he was playing many of his hits.

The call to Kool & the Gang was to extend an invitation to play the show. It would have been one of the largest audiences we'd played for up to that point, and that meant great international exposure, but we had to decline. It was a great opportunity, but we were in the middle of a project and things were going well. To abandon at that point would have made it much harder to pick it up again. It was more productive to get everything recorded without taking a break, because that could impact the creative process, and we didn't want to risk that. But the calls didn't stop. Elton himself called and asked if we'd do it as a favor, and the group finally agreed to participate.

It was apparent that he was grateful for our presence, because he was waiting outside of the stadium to greet us as we drove up.

Of course, the stadium was sold out, and Elton couldn't have been more gracious and complimentary. It was also great exposure for us, because it was being recorded and broadcast around the world. Our song list included lots of hits: "Ladies' Night," "Hollywood Swinging," "Tonight," "Too Hot," "Jones vs. Jones," "(When You Say You Love Somebody) in the Heart," "Take My Heart," "Joanna," "Get Down on It," "Let's Go Dancin'," and of course "Celebration." It was the beginning of a great friendship between Kool & the Gang and Sir Elton John.

After a successful show, we returned to the studio. Fortunately, we were able to pick up where we left off and quickly finished recording the album. Then, in November of that year, we were in London visiting the Phonogram office where we ran into Bob Geldof, humanitarian and lead singer of the Boomtown Rats. He created a group called Band Aid to include many popular artists who would contribute to a single and video called "Do They Know It's Christmas?" Kool & the Gang was invited to participate. The song debuted in December and quickly sold over 2.5 million copies while the video, packed with mostly UK stars, was in endless rotation on MTV. The high-profile project was in support of a charity created to combat the famine in Ethiopia. Other artists in attendance included George Michael, Paul Young, Boy George, Bono, Duran Duran, Phil Collins, Sting, and Jody Watley.

To the surprise of our naysayers, *Emergency* went on to crush the charts with four huge hits. Just when we thought that "Celebration" would probably be our biggest song, along came tracks like "Emergency," "Fresh," "Misled," and "Cherish." Jim was back to help with production, and that combination proved that lightning could strike twice.

That was our sixteenth album, and it went on to be our biggest seller, going double platinum. In 1985 we made history as the only band with four top-twenty singles on the same album. It was a testament to our craftsmanship and dedication that we'd been grinding since the late '60s, and here we were, making hits almost two decades later.

Two years later we were back with *Forever*, and that album yielded two hits, "Victory" and "Stone Love," along with the songs "Peace-maker," "Holiday," and "Special Way."

Throughout the '80s we adjusted to the new trends in music, MTV, and videos, and that certainly helped expose our songs to a wider audience. Of course, we'd been on many TV and variety shows by that point, but most of our videos were live performances with creative storytelling.

I loved doing the videos, but it was tiring, because they often took a long time to film and, to be honest, some of the concepts didn't make a lot of sense to me. We brought in directors, and they shared their vision, proposed shooting locations and, once chosen, took care of the details. We filmed "Get Down on It" in the New York subway, and they actually stopped the trains so we could shoot the video. On some of those videos, I thought the concept was strange or that there was too much going on. Some were very experimental, but as usual I went with the flow.

The video for "Emergency" was the one that first brought us to MTV. Before that we'd submitted plenty of them, but they didn't really get played. It took a while before MTV routinely integrated African American artists other than Michael Jackson or Diana Ross into the rotation. "Emergency" had more of a rock flavor, and that must have helped it get airplay. It was not expected, but in a way it was typical of our approach. Kool & the Gang always had a different sound—a jazzy, funky sound, different rhythms—and we liked to change it up. No matter what genre of song we created, it had our unmistakable vibe. One thing was for sure, it felt good to be back on top again.

The problem was that when I first wrote the song "Emergency," the others in the band weren't responding to it, which happened with all of us. I felt strongly about it, so I took it to our music director, Curtis Williams, and played two versions for him, one with a funk vibe and the other with a rock flavor that opened with a guitar solo. He loved the rock version best, and that's what we went with.

It's similar to how, back in 1981, I wrote a few lines of the song "Take My Heart (You Can Have It If You Want It)" and gave it to J.T. He said, "Man, I like this." Then he added his section. We had a smooth way of collaborating. Again, the rest of the band wasn't feeling it, but we released it, and it went to number one on the charts.

That happened a few times: I began the process, and some of the others might not have felt the song. I got a sense of satisfaction when it charted, because it validated the talent I felt was in me to create songs people would respond to. I learned not to doubt my instincts or discount my talent when it came to songwriting.

Seeing that the rock flavor worked for us, Khalis led the process to write "Misled" with J.T., and the other songs on that album followed suit. This moved us into the rock 'n' roll stage of our career as we continued morphing with the ever-changing music taste of our fans. It must have been the right direction for us at that time, because that album ended up being our biggest seller.

Changing up our sound worked wonders for us, and our career continued to explode. Doing that helped raise our profile with not only fans but also our peers. That success started us on the path toward working with Bryan Adams, Van Halen, Elton John, and later Dave Matthews, Kid Rock, and many others.

Ladies' Night

I certainly had my share of fun on the road while I was between marriages, but I was probably considered tame by most accounts. It's not that I didn't have plenty of good times, because I did. I suppose that's one of the perks of celebrity, the attention that comes with it. I'm not going to lie; it can be addicting. I've seen many artists worship at the altar of stardom, both men and women.

Just as my career was kicking off, I married my first wife. It was 1970, and we were just too young. That's all there is to it. Our interests changed as we grew up. I went in the music direction, and she went her way. I wrote the song "Too Hot" about my experiences falling in love so young and how painful a breakup can be. But out of that union came my first two wonderful sons, Dorian and Jorge.

My next marriage was in 1987. Naturally, I met her while I was on tour—where I spent most of my time, when I wasn't recording. She was Japanese, and we had a son named Gregory, who is now a great success as a musician in Japan.

Next came the '90s and another marriage. That one was in 1995 to a Vietnamese woman, and we have two children, Jordan and Aaron.

So from those unions, I have five children, all boys. They are the treasured result of all my relationships. While the union can fade, the children remain as a reminder of the best of two people, and that's how I feel about each of my boys. We talk all the time, and I've always been involved in their lives. Because of my profession, I couldn't be with them all the time, but we had special moments. I enjoy how our relationships have evolved as they've become adults with their own families. They are each doing well in their chosen fields, and I try to help them make smart choices.

Sometimes, I struggle to make sense of marriage and divorce. We all know relationships are complicated, to say the least. Being successful in this industry just compounds the issues. My mother used to equate relationships to holidays. "Every day is Christmas when you have someone." I knew what she was saying. You should have a feeling of excitement and joy when you are with your person. Naturally, it can fade with time, but you should still have those feelings deep inside. If you don't, that's a problem.

I don't know what it's like to be with the same person for a life-time, something that was more common when I was coming up. Then I wonder, is it worth it if you feel like you are settling just because you don't want to disrupt the marriage? Of course, many couples last for decades, and it works for them. It's just not something I experienced. Maybe that was because of the temptations from the road, the eternal questions of *What if?* or *Is there more?*

Even when I was in a committed relationship, it was never easy, because of the travel and attention. We'd have to schedule when I would be home, knowing that it wouldn't be for long. When a band is in demand, you have to take advantage of that, and that's what we did. And we still do to this day.

That professional dedication is the key to our band's ability to navigate wavering musical tastes, but the element that never changes, regardless of record sales, is the availability of women. There is never a shortage of temptation, of opportunity, regardless of one's relation-ship status.

That element of band life is undeniably ubiquitous, and I knew that at the beginning of my career. Hell, I looked forward to it, antici-pated it, but I was in a relationship, so I initially enjoyed it from afar. I enjoyed the attention and celebration of my craft, the payoff after hours upon hours of practice.

Yet as my personal life wended its way through its own inevitable machinations, so too did my yearning for appreciation and validation. I'd never considered the fact that my needs would fluctuate as my relationship status changed, but they did. When my first marriage was over, Kool & the Gang was becoming even more popular and visible, in large part because of the videos that played regularly on music programs and in heavy rotation on MTV.

One thing that has never changed is that I love all types of women. I see the beauty and the godliness in everyone. So if I see a woman whom I find attractive, it doesn't matter about the skin tone or racial makeup. I've never been concerned about cultural pressures to date only within my race. I think the bonds of love circumvent the baked-in notions we might have of people based on race, skin color, or culture. Traveling the world for so many years, I've encountered women from countless cultures, and for me it's about the ability to open myself to experiences without confining that to a specific type. To that point, while I've dated many races, most of my longer relationships have been with Asian women.

Maybe because of that openness, I've remained friends with all the women I dated or married from around the world. That might sound impossible or delusional on my part, but it's true. I still hear from many of them when they call just to catch up. It's a way for us to share the good times we had without having to worry about the issues. Now that we are not together, that's off the table, and we can focus on a genuine friendship.

I suppose it's only natural to think about "the one that got away," or wonder what my life would have been like if I'd made different choices in partners to be with for the long term. Who knows, and now, does it matter anyway?

Once, we were on a sold-out tour with a stop in Australia. We'd just finished touring on a bill with the Jacksons, Sister Sledge, and the Pointer Sisters, but we were back on the road. That's one of the amazing things about the band. We are loved no matter where we go, and the audiences still come out. It's amazing.

So on that tour, I was in my hotel room smoking a little weed and writing songs on the piano, because I'm always cooking up some new music. Our road manager called and said, "We need to go down to the club for an appearance and some autographs, publicity stuff."

I wasn't feeling it, because I was in the music zone and didn't want to stop. "I'm going to sit this one out," I told him.

"You got to go. We need you down there. Come on!"

I got dressed, brushed my teeth, made sure I couldn't smell any weed on me, and headed to the club. The manager was waiting at the entrance and led me to the VIP area. While I was in the club, this young lady came in. And I never do this, but I said, "Wow, you look really lovely this evening." It was totally out of character—I'm never that forward. It's just not me.

She came back and said, "What's the rest of it?"

I paid her a few more compliments, and then she went downstairs to dance. I also headed to the dance floor and met a girl named Novera, who was also gorgeous. Then I went over to the young lady I had followed to the dance floor and found out her name was Roxanne. She and Novera were friends. I don't know what it was, but Roxanne felt like "the one," the love of my life.

After I finished with my band duties, I asked for Roxanne's number, got a cab, and went back to the hotel to finish my weed and play the piano. Then I went to get her phone number out of my pocket, and it wasn't there! I couldn't find the number! *Oh, shit!* I got back in a taxi, and I asked the driver, "Please take me to the club." I went downstairs, and she was still there.

"I lost your number," I told her.

"You came back for me?"

"Uh, yes, I did."

"Well, here's my number again."

"Can I take you to dinner tomorrow? Is that cool?"

The next night, we had an amazing dinner at an Indian restaurant. She said she had a great time, and the conversation just flowed. I found out she was of Mauritian descent, from the African island nation of Mauritius. It's a multiethnic country of Indian, African, Chinese, and French origins. It was one of those evenings that I lost all track of time, all my attention focused on the intriguing young lady in front of me.

I kissed her at the end of the night, and to this day I still remember what that was like. It was so passionate, and I felt such a connection with her. I guess it was a spark or instant chemistry. Whatever it was, I loved that feeling and didn't want to lose it.

After the Australian tour, I came back to the States and invited her to visit. She agreed and ended up coming to several of our shows around the country. Sometimes, we returned to Australia, and I holed up in the apartment I'd rented for her.

Our relationship blossomed and the love felt real, true, and good. I thought, *This is it! This is what everyone's been talking about. The love of your life. Your soulmate.* After a couple of marriages, many encounters, and fleeting relationships, I had found my person. That feeling of relief washed over me as I realized there would always be someone waiting for me after a gig or a long night in the studio. I can't tell you how difficult it was to find a woman who understood my life and could handle the issues that come with it.

We were in Málaga, Spain, for yet another world tour. We stepped into a nightclub owned by an arms dealer who flew in beautiful women from all over the world for entertainment purposes. We were having a great time when Roxanne turned to me and said, "I'm going back to Australia, because I'm living your life, not mine. I have to do me now."

I was caught completely off guard. I'd always felt like an intuitive person, someone who was good at reading people and following my instincts. The fact that I never had any idea that she was unhappy had me feeling a certain kind of way. Yet again my career had blinded me to what was going on in my life with this wonderful woman.

It made me sad, because we'd had deep, intense conversations. I was friends with her mother, father, and brother, and I even stayed at their place when I was in the UK. Roxanne and I had picked out the name Jordan for our future son. That's how deep we got. Her mother pulled me aside and said, "I know Roxanne, and you're definitely the guy for her."

As I always do, I wrote a song about the experience and called it "In Too Deep." Sometimes, I look at songs like that one and "Too Hot" and wonder what it means to have a good relationship. Is it all just fodder for my craft? Grist for the musical mill? Am I resigned to a life filled with unsuccessful relationships marked by songs with an undertone of sadness and regret?

To make matters worse, the band was in a state of transition. Musically, we weren't where we wanted to be. In the late '80s the band rehearsed at Prince's Paisley Park, with Paula Abdul helping to finesse our choreography before we embarked on a fifty-city US tour. At the end of that tour, we were greeted with the news that J.T., our lead singer, the voice of many hits, was leaving for a solo career. He'd come down with what we called L.S.S., a common band disease, Lead Singer Syndrome.

Something happens to everyone when they become successful, especially in show business—not just lead singers but all of us. There are changes in demeanor, subtle at first, but it just comes with the territory. Some folks get carried away with themselves. Success can change even the humblest people. When I was living on Gramercy, one of the guys parked his old car across the street by a construction site. When we all went out to his car, we saw that a construction beam had fallen on it. Someone said, "Don't worry. It looks better anyway." The next thing you know, we're driving a Mercedes or a Bentley. It changes you. We called it "getting new." Once folks reach a certain level, they might feel more entitled to say or do things they wouldn't have done before.

On the road J.T. and I were often roommates and had a great relationship. We went to the clubs together and then promised each other our antics would stay between us. We shared a brotherhood. Without him I wasn't sure how many times the band could reinvent itself. Yet there was no denying Kool & the Gang's staying power.

With the release of the album *Sweat*, we'd gone more of a synth-pop R&B route. It was tough, because we were trying to find our place without the singer who had been with us throughout the '80s. There were two singles—"Raindrops" and "Never Give Up"—but they didn't perform as well as our past records. In 1993 came the album *Unite* (also known as *Jump Up on It!*), but things seemed to be turning around in 1996 when J.T. returned to cut the record *State of Affairs*. Unfortunately, the public's musical tastes had changed, and the album didn't find the large audience the others had.

What we had on our side was the wide appeal of the music we had created for the past two decades. Our fans were a variety of different types of folks early on, because our first album hit the R&B and pop charts. That opened us up to a large fan base that continued to grow. We drew fans who knew we were Black, but we found a large Caucasian audience as well.

Some of the early '70s hits like "Jungle Boogie" kept our fans of funk coming back, and that was followed by "Hollywood Swinging." When "Open Sesame" made the *Saturday Night Fever* soundtrack, we were about as mainstream as a group can get. The movie and soundtrack were such a powerhouse that people who might not have listened to us before got a taste of our style.

The hits of the '80s brought us to a mainstream audience, regardless of race, because songs like "Ladies' Night" and "Too Hot" had such a wide appeal. That popularity was only solidified when the anthem "Celebration" and ballads like "Joanna" shot through stereo speakers around the world.

Being included in other popular films, such as *Rocky*, *Pulp Fiction*, and *Wreck-It Ralph*, helped us reach younger generations. That opened us up to DJs and the prolific sampling of many of Kool & the Gang's songs.

So by the late '90s, even though some albums didn't perform as we had hoped, our catalog of hits kept the live shows in demand around the world. Everywhere we went—Sri Lanka, India, Germany—it didn't matter the culture or the demographic makeup; they knew our songs and sang along. We went to places with predominantly Caucasian audiences of a hundred thousand, and the response was always the same. It showed how important it was to have consistent, timeless hits, and the perseverance to keep the band going.

Talk to Me

Our family had recently moved to Los Angeles, where I went through my first divorce. As one of the conditions, I was required to enroll in an anger management course, and at first that made me, well, angry.

All I had done was squeeze her arm when we were arguing, and she filed charges. The cops showed up with guns drawn, and of course, they just saw this tall Black man standing in front of them. They took me down to the station, and the man at the desk said, "Hey, I know who you are." It felt good to at least get some decent treatment during the ordeal. Then he said, "I think we can let you leave on your own recognizance."

Not too long after, we were ordered to attend arbitration, and the session was to take place at the courthouse. As I was driving, I got a call.

"Mr. Brown?"

"Yes?"

"Don't go to the courthouse."

I said, "OK, but I'm on my way. I'm meeting my wife."

He said, "We'd like you to come in the secure entrance. It's more discreet."

I was then directed to a nondescript entrance that was apparently used by all the rambunctious celebrities in Los Angeles as a way to avoid tabloids and paparazzi.

When I got to the private conference room, my wife was waiting there with the children. There were toys available to keep the kids occupied while we talked. It was a surprisingly nice room, and the atmosphere was one of compromise and cooperation.

Our attorneys were with us, and they said, "OK, George, tell us ten things you like about your wife." So of course I complied. Then it was her turn. "Tell us ten things you like about George." Next we were both asked to tell "ten things you dislike about the other person."

After we finished, they went off to deliberate in private. It was all very civil and surprisingly calm. To be honest, it felt almost like a business deal, as if we were negotiating the price of a new car or purchasing a home.

Next we went in front of the judge for the decision. My attorney talked with the judge in a hushed whisper. The judge then called me to approach the bench. "Hello, Mr. Brown," he said. "Let's get this taken care of right away." Then he motioned to the bailiff. The bailiff approached the desk and talked to the judge and my attorney. Then he turned to me and said, "Let's get out of here. You can go."

I went through a similar incident where my lawyer said, "The judge is quite cranky today. He's throwing the book at everyone. Let's see what we can do." He spoke with the judge sotto voce, and I was allowed to leave. I turned to my lawyer and said, "Well, obviously, you've got to know when to play and when to fold."

Over the following months, I held my end of the bargain and attended therapy, and I'll admit that it was beneficial. It was less about anger and more about understanding human nature and how to effectively communicate with others, no matter who they are. My therapist became a good friend, and by the end of it, he found me to be "mellow and jokey." It was a side that the court doesn't see, because they just move from one case to the next.

Those sessions helped me peel back the layers and learn more about myself. If I was touring, I'd call in from on the road for my weekly session.

"Where are you this time, George?" my therapist would ask.

"I'm in Helsinki, Finland."

"It must be really late there."

"Yes, it is," I said. "Plus, I have to leave at 6:00 AM for the next show."

"OK, then let's get to it. How are things going?"

Having those sessions while I was working was almost more difficult than attending them in person, because I was besieged by the stresses of a tour. I have trouble sleeping anyway, but in that particular case, I knew that I needed rest before the three-hour ride to the next concert, which was at a festival; a festival brings along its own set of challenges. In Europe the weather can be alarmingly dismal. It rains a lot, and it can get rather cold.

Being in the middle of a field somewhere in bad weather—sometimes even having to take a ferry to reach the site—adds so much more to the process of playing in a band. If I couldn't fall asleep, I dreaded the moment the road manager would bang on the door. "Just get up, take your shower, and bring your stuff right back down to the lobby, because we gotta go soon."

To add to that, I had these counseling sessions where it was almost impossible not to be frustrated with all the hassles that come with a tour. The sessions helped me learn to appreciate those times and put things into perspective. That enabled me to grow as a person and remember to slow down and appreciate what I'd worked for all those years.

I also learned a lot about relationships and how just one person is rarely at fault. It's more a culmination of events, a realization that the life that was once shared peacefully has evolved into an unhealthy union. And that's OK. We have a mind-set that divorce is a failure, but I don't see it that way, especially if there are children. How can that be a failure?

Something that bothered me was the obvious preferential treatment that people in the public eye receive that most others do not. If I'd been a brother from Compton with a low-paying job or no job at all, things would have quickly gone left. I sure as hell wouldn't have been ordered to counseling that could take place by phone as I traveled around the world to entertain cheering crowds.

Money makes things happen, even if it's not a conscious choice. We always said in the band, "Life is a shit sandwich, so you'd better have plenty of bread."

A Lesson in Collaboration

To me, that's what Kool & the Gang has always been: a band made up of survivors, musical shapeshifters. No matter what obstacles we came up against, we were able to pull together, collaborate, and make great music. Maybe every song wasn't a hit, but we were consistently putting out quality music for our fans while reaching new listeners with the chart-toppers. That was a smart way to grow our band and our brand year after year. The goal for all of us was always longevity. Music was our way of life, and it still is. I understood that we couldn't expect to create number-one hits every time, but if we were able to keep hitting the charts, we'd be able to sustain our popularity and, thus, our careers.

I always strove to better my craft. In the beginning, I studied the drums. Later I even tried to attend the Manhattan School of Music. They said I'd have to learn the kettle drums, because a snare drum was referred to as just the side piece in classical music. You were required to play an instrument that had intervals, from C to E and E to G, for example. Then you would perform an audition, but I didn't get the chance, because the group became so successful and, fortunately, took over my life.

Songwriting always came easy for me, and it felt natural. I got inspired walking down the streets of New York, touring around the world, and going through my relationships. Writing the music was also a natural fit, so I experimented with various sounds until it felt just right. With "Ladies' Night," we'd moved away from straight funk and embraced the dance/disco sound, which worked for that song. Quincy Jones said something along the lines of "You don't want to be too far in the past or too far ahead. You want to be now." He's right. It's a delicate balance.

Collaboration is a learned skill for most creatives. When we write, compose, arrange, or otherwise work on our art, it's usually internal, a solitary process. So working with others can be a challenge. In the beginning, we worked together more freely, because we were searching for our sound, the direction the band would take. We all had talent, and it was helpful to get input from everyone, because our differences are what made us unique.

With success came a tremendous amount of pressure to keep the hits coming. To our credit, we were able to successfully move from one musical genre to another, something that doesn't happen often. In the process we had to learn to listen to each other and not let our preconceived notions inform the decision-making: "He only writes ballads," or "Those lyrics are whack."

We had to learn to recognize that we had all grown and changed and matured in our musical abilities. Having a producer act as a sounding board also helped, since no matter how hard we tried, sometimes we couldn't get out of our own way. Having the opinion of a professional we trusted helped us get past the bullshit and focus on the work.

Despite the many challenges, I've always felt honored and blessed to be able to make music for so long. It's the American dream to be able to do what you enjoy and make a living at it. Music has been a constant throughout my life, and I've always focused on improving my craft for the betterment of the group, and the betterment of myself.

4

CHORUS

———

DRUMMERS HAVE A REPUTATION for wanting to step out from behind the kit. Dennis Wilson of the Beach Boys, Don Henley of the Eagles, Dave Grohl from Nirvana, Phil Collins with Genesis, and Questlove from the Roots are all examples of men who stepped away from the drums at some point in their career. We can't forget the women either: Karen Carpenter, Danielle Haim, Belinda Carlisle, and of course Sheila E. started on drums before moving to lead singer.

I followed a similar path, but with a twist. I did the same thing in my group by moving on to the keyboard and other instruments, especially during the time of synth-pop and recorded drumbeats. That felt like a way for me to do more than drums and songwriting, and to play other instruments and share the duties of the band, especially on tours. By then J.T. had left for the second time. He first departed in 1988 but returned briefly in 1996, but the old magic wasn't there. Khalis and Spike left and returned, and several other lineup changes had taken place.

During that time we had a manager who, no matter what you did, he'd done it better. That was just his personality. If you had a

Lamborghini, he had three. One day I was driving down Lincoln Boulevard in Los Angeles. I'd just dropped off my girlfriend, Roxanne, at the airport so she could return to Australia, and I was brokenhearted. As I drove back to Marina del Rey, the phone rang. It was the manager.

"The guys don't like your attitude," he said bluntly.

I was stunned. J.T. had recently left again after an underperforming album, so it didn't seem to me like the right time to make even more changes. "My attitude?" I said. "I'm a founding member. I've been here from day one."

"They want you to step off the road for a while."

What the hell? I was stunned. I'd noticed some crazy shit going on, like my costumes for a show would be missing, little things like that, but I didn't anticipate being sidelined from the tour. Some of the Kool & the Gang team would tell people, "George is difficult to get along with and overly critical." Then I met them and always heard how easygoing I was. Some of the criticism was true: I could be critical, but that was focused on the music, not my bandmates. My frustration sometimes came from the fact that no one understood that I did much more than play drums. Songwriting, playing piano, singing, arranging—all those tasks weren't discussed, because it was easier to keep me pigeonholed as "the drummer."

How could I get around that and make myself heard? I wrote good songs. I made good music, and that did all the talking for me. When Deodato was our producer, he took everyone's input and guided us toward what was best for the band, not our egos. That helped my songs get accepted based purely on their strength, not ego. Not even mine.

It was status quo for the band to reinvent itself, not only musically but also with a shakeup of its members. My situation was a little different. I had been there from the beginning. I was an integral part of the machine, a hard worker, a contributor, a founder. I could play not just drums but also percussion, piano, and keyboard. I could wear many musical hats, if you will. Plus, I consistently contributed to the songwriting for many of the Kool & the Gang hits.

Let's face it: bands have turmoil that leads to changes and reorgs, much like any business. It's just that this business is entertainment. So it wasn't like I felt like I was owed a place, but I did feel like I'd earned it by putting in the work. Even personality-wise, I had tumultuous periods, but they were mild in comparison to most artists. My main focus was always on the work. I enjoyed the recreational benefits that came along with it, but only to a degree and rarely to excess.

My parents instilled in me persistence and a solid work ethic. Plus, of course, it was much more than just a job for me—and most musicians. I do it because I love it and because I have to. Making music is part of me, so that informs my work and makes it much more pleasurable, because I am blessed to be able to do something I truly enjoy.

The reality is that working together for years can be difficult for any band. Everyone has agendas. As you grow older, people have families and other people get involved, and that is in addition to the band's growth. What takes priority? And who decides?

There's no denying that the '80s were a great time for the band, but it was tough as well. Until that time, we were struggling to maintain our hard-earned success. In the '80s we achieved fame, but it came at a price. By that time we had our own priorities. There were a lot of egos and jealousy and, frankly, a lot of nonsense. Of course, it wasn't just within our band; the decade of excess impacted each of us in different ways.

White powder was inescapable. Cocaine was everywhere. The party atmosphere was expected and accepted, business as usual, de rigueur. It was part of the culture that evolved out of the disco craze. Glitzy, stylish cop shows on TV like *Miami Vice* and general mainstream acceptance of overindulgence fueled the misconception that everyone was partying and it was harmless fun. The good times will never fade. Pass the bottle and give me the joint. Bring the women over here. Wine, women, and cocaine.

Our band had its share of craziness, but somehow most of it went under the publicity radar. Our antics weren't splashed across the gossip papers like they were for many other groups, so our reputation as a harmless party band remained intact. With the addition of J.T. as lead singer, we were propelled into the musical stratosphere, but it took some adjustment. At first, fans called him T.J. for some reason.

"Where is T.J.?" fans asked.

Some of us responded, "I'm all the T.J. you need."

The character of the person evolves, sometimes gradually and sometimes quickly, and I'm no exception. I think some people just get carried away with themselves and take it to the extreme. I'd look at them and think, "Man. This guy used to have a beat-up car and ten dollars to his name."

When we struggled, we might have wanted to say "fuck you" to each other, but we didn't. We bit our tongues and focused on the work. When we reached superstar status, it was a different story. Suddenly, it was easy to say "fuck you" to anyone and everyone. Maybe it was the money or the attention—probably both—but success gives people a certain sense of entitlement. T.J. (or J.T.) came in at that time, so it was a difficult situation.

Just like any business, when a band is made up of family members, it adds a different level of complexity. We had two brothers, a manager who was a first cousin, and spouses who were involved, all basically connected to the same family. Sometimes, their priorities might have been different from other members of the band, so it could complicate many decisions, especially where money was involved.

I made a habit of retaining an outside attorney and other team members to help look after my interests, because they might not be the same as the band's interests. That's just the way it is. I accept it, and I've learned how to work with it. If I want my material to get some traction, I need an advocate supporting my interests. So I learned to make my own way.

Having the outside influences of T.J./J.T. and Deodato gave us the ability to see things from different perspectives. Though we were able to create good music within the band, bringing in other talented people took us to a different level.

Sometimes I had to fight to get my music heard by the group, and I'm glad I did. When I wrote "Too Hot," they didn't believe in it. It wasn't on the funk side, so the consensus was that it wouldn't work. Not only that, when Deodato said we should try it, they went along with it but didn't want any writing credit. They said, "Oh, no, you keep it. You wrote it all." Then it turned out to be a multiplatinum record, and their interest changed.

The same thing happened with the song "Emergency." I made it rock 'n' roll, then MTV played it, and sales went through the roof. I'm not saying my instincts were always right and no one else contributed, but I did have to fight to be heard, and we all benefited from those hits.

When I was kicked off the tour, I wondered if the fact that I'd been through anger management years ago was being used against me. That was the only thing that made sense to me. Therapy makes it easier to label someone, which is exactly the opposite of what should happen. Perceived weakness can be used against someone, because there was a history, even though I'd grown as a result. Was it the band or the manager? I didn't know what to believe, but the fact was that I'd been benched.

So in the late '90s, there I was with the love of my life headed back to Australia, and I was sidelined from the band that I helped create. If it weren't for the fact that I had written a lot of the music, I wouldn't have had the royalty income during those years. That would have been financially disastrous for me.

Physical Health

It was time for me to reassess. My health came first. Since moving to California in the mid-'80s, I'd become more and more immersed in healthy living, and it was important for me to focus on myself. I'd been a vegetarian and then a vegan for many years, and I took that further by experimenting with juicing and other diets. Physically, I got more serious about working out and trying other sports, eventually earning a black belt in karate.

Medically, I put more focus on checkups and doctor visits. I also experimented with the plethora of options in the health industry, especially in California. I began getting vitamin IV drips. I also tried blood purification and deep-tissue massages.

My spiritual journey continued as well. I've always been interested in the transcendental arts and meditation, and even in employing the services of intuitive counselors and healers for advice and guidance, like my friend Linda, a metaphysical clinician.

With the unplanned professional downtime, I felt like it was the perfect opportunity to put focus on the other areas of my life. Endless touring can be immensely rewarding, but it's not easy to maintain a healthy regimen, although I certainly tried. Everywhere we went, I hunted down the restaurants with vegetarian options. Back in the day, the choices were sparse, but fortunately they became more popular as vegetarian living caught on.

Being out of the band was also a time to reexamine my career and what I wanted to do. Over the years, I was offered several opportunities to explore other projects, including writing, playing, and singing my own material. I gave it some thought each time, but I really wanted to keep my focus on the band. I had devoted more than three decades to cranking out hits that fed the musical beast that was Kool & the Gang—more songs, more hits, more tours. I put my best songwriting, my best playing, and all my time into that. I'd worked all my life to be in that spot, and I'd made it. I also had a wife and children to support at the time, and that didn't leave a lot of time for anything else.

Before I moved on, I thought about the times others had commented on my talent and the contributions I made to the industry. We were playing in London, and Marvin Gaye came out of his self-imposed exile to see us. When we finished playing, he walked over and said, "Man, you really can play some drums." Of course, he was a former drummer, so it felt good to hear that. I used to play his records all day long while smoking herb and drinking cognac. It was my way to relax.

Morris Day, the lead singer of the Time, is a good friend, and he started as a drummer as well. We were walking down the street one day, and he said, "Man, if it wasn't for you, George, none of us would be doing this today. You're the captain. You did this, and that's why we are able to do it." It was comforting to hear that.

Now the situation was different. My priorities had shifted, because doing what I loved was no longer an option, at least not how I'd been doing it. But it wasn't a time to relax; it was my time to explore my talents in my own way. My son Gregory started hunting for storefronts about four blocks from Inglewood in a mall on Truxton Avenue. One day he told me he'd found something.

"Which place did you find?" I asked.

"Come take a look. I think this one will work."

I checked it out, and it was just what I needed. I sourced the materials and the skilled labor necessary to begin building a studio, and it was ready in just a few weeks. Music producer Preston Glass was a good friend who taught extension courses at UCLA. He asked me to teach a few classes, and when I told him about my new studio, he referred Ali-Ollie Woodson of the Temptations, who became the first person to record there. I started off working with people like Joanne "Jojo" McDuffie, lead singer of the Mary Jane Girls, the group created by Rick James, and Debra Laws, who had a big hit in the '80s with "Very Special." Other initial clients were a member of the Manhattans and the British R&B group Loose Ends.

What a godsend! I'd always written and produced, but to work with new people invigorated my creativity and exposed me to different musical styles and fresh ideas. It felt so rewarding to have my own musical space, where others felt as safe and comfortable as I did. I was getting better and better as a producer, but I didn't stop there. I studied voice with Seth Riggs, an acclaimed vocal coach who worked with artists like Stevie Wonder, Prince, and Michael Jackson. Having the dedicated space honed my writing chops, my vocal chops, and my production chops. It meant so much because, for the first time, it was all me.

I collaborated with some great professionals who helped out, and it felt amazing. Experienced musicians like Lewis Taylor; Ricky Rouse (Funkadelic, Chaka Khan); Phil Brown (Pat Benatar, Steve Perry); Jimmy Macon (the Gap Band); Wah Wah Watson (Jackson 5, Gladys Knight, the Pointer Sisters); and Romeo Williams (Elton John) were eager to pitch in. (When Romeo passed, he left me a mixing board that I keep in the studio to this day as a tribute to him.)

One day I was at Meryl's Music, near Santa Monica, buying equipment for my studio. Meryl said, "George, run upstairs. There's somebody I want you to see." I went upstairs, and there was a jovial guy named Bill Augustine.

"Play something! Play something," he said.

I smiled. "Well, actually, I'd like to learn jazz harmony. I can play pop on the piano, but I'm self-taught. I'd like to see if I can learn more."

I started working with him on my piano playing and music reading, both of which improved. It broadened my skills so much that one time, after I'd rejoined the band on tour, we were on a TV show in Germany, I was on piano with the show's full orchestra.

They gave me the sheet music and a chord chart. The full band played the melody. I saw that the chord changes were jazz chords, and I could play them.

The other members of Kool & the Gang were folded into the band, and thanks to the training I'd done, I had no problem keeping up. It felt amazing, so much so that I went on to study classical piano. In jazz, most of the time you get the lead sheet with the chords and the melody, but in classical you're reading the treble clef, the bass clef, and the full staff, instead of the treble staff with the chords on top. You're reading the bass for the left hand and the treble for the right hand. They are completely different.

The synchronicity of the bass clef is a step lower, so if I were playing B, which is the third line on the treble staff, it is on the second line of the bass staff. I have a buddy who plays saxophone, and he also took lessons with Bill. He said, "Good luck with that synchronicity."

When I was out of the band, I used those years off the road to improve myself personally and professionally.

The Beat Goes On

In 2004 Khalis and I were up in San Jose at a Kool & the Gang show. There we were, two guys who helped start the band, sitting in the audience watching J.T. sing as the band played our songs. We attended a couple of shows, and at one of them, I went backstage, and they said, "You could have come back whenever you wanted. Join us on tour." And just like that, I was back in the band after a seven-year exile.

I was glad to be where I felt most at home. Being back with the band, I felt like I had more of a voice, but it still took a while for me to get production credit. I finally spoke up and said, "I produced a lot of this stuff along with Khalis." Finally, they relented, and now I had my recording studio as well. Looking back, it felt strange to be out of a band I helped create, but I learned not to be angry or upset. I always knew that was my place, where I belonged. Now it keeps getting better. And that break allowed me to create a business that I can continue when Kool & the Gang is off the road. So somehow it all worked out as it was supposed to.

Sometimes, the universe will motivate you by taking away something comfortable to give you the kick in the ass you need. The blessing is that I'm a creative being. I love being with people, but I'm also a private person. Those quiet, introspective moments are when I write my best work. I love performing, but it's not about stardom or attention for me. We've been successful since we were teenagers. That newness wears off, and as you grow, you can hype yourself up so much that the focus is on you instead of the performance, where it should be. Then you settle into it, censoring yourself and controlling your emotions. You get to the point of enjoying the audience, whether it's an intimate setting or half a million people at a stadium.

West Coast Vibes

I love the East Coast, but one thing that I enjoy about living in Los Angeles is the proximity to so many artists. I've lived in the Hollywood Hills and Marina del Rey right on the ocean. What beautiful places! My wife and I have been in our current house for twenty-two years, and we've continued to make changes to suit our needs, including my in-home studio.

Rick James lived down the street and often made his way to my studio to hang out. Every time I parked my Range Rover at the nearby Ralphs supermarket, Rick's friend Val Young, who had solo hits and sang with the Mary Jane Girls, came in looking for him. She'd find me and say, "Oh, it's only you, George. I saw the Range Rover and thought maybe Rick was here!" That's what our neighborhood is like.

It still keeps me up to date on the current music trends, because I often run into new artists.

Mike Campbell, a member of Tom Petty's band, the Heartbreakers, lives nearby, and Akon is a couple of houses down from me. My housekeeper works with other families in the neighborhood, and one year she brought my kids the Halloween costumes they wanted but had not been able to find.

The costumes were from Mick and Bianca Jagger's daughter, who lived down the street. She just asked, "Please bring them back in good condition, because Granddad gave this to us." It's an interesting neighborhood to be sure.

Oddly enough, it's rather peaceful, which I wouldn't have imagined Los Angeles could be. It reminds me of living in the country. If I go two blocks over, I can get on the boulevard, but the noise is so well buffered that I can't hear it at home.

Finding a place where I feel comfortable helps me to be at peace with myself, and that allows me to be more creative. Of course, my kids like their own type of music, and I can appreciate new artists, but I try not to let their style influence my music too much. That's one thing I stress with not only Kool & the Gang but also any musicians who create their material. I encourage them to focus on music that is appropriate for their age group; otherwise, it can come off as disingenuous.

For example, "Too Hot" is a story of coming into enlightenment about relationships and high school sweethearts coming into their own as adults. It's about that realization that the attraction may only be "young love." It's about developing the understanding that people sometimes grow and change, and that can affect relationships.

The song "Cherish" came out in 1984, and we were in our midthirties. The theme was more mature, with the focus on someone dying and what that means. *If you should die, will I make it?* It's about being age appropriate, because when you're true to yourself, genuine creativity comes to life. It's all about professional growth. It's about having the curiosity to continue learning and honing your craft.

Sometimes, I'm working late in the studio and think, *Wow, this is sounding great.* Then I go back the next day and realize, *Man, I got to fix that.* Sometimes it's a recent track, and sometimes it's one from weeks ago. I come back and listen to it and think it's right for a film I'm scoring or an artist I'm working with, but it has to make sense and not feel forced.

The creative process has always not just interested me but consumed me, if I'm being honest. With "Too Hot," I was smoking lots of herb, which is tough on a singing voice but can be helpful creatively, because it opens the mind to other possibilities. At least it does for me. Now I'm more drawn to edibles to preserve my vocals.

Sometimes, when I'm playing the piano and writing music, it feels like my hands are moving by themselves. It's as if the writing is automatic. The creativity just consumes me, and I can't control it, nor do I want to. I let it come to its natural conclusion. The result might be genius or a rough draft, but it always surprises me.

Not that it happens all the time, but if everything is in place, the work comes to life. Sometimes I might not even like what comes out, but it is always a growing experience. Maybe it's attributed to working with young people, listening to streaming services, and being with my kids. I can see the changes in my work, and I give thanks for it. I see the progression and growth while still being true to what resonates with me.

Sometimes, I'll hear songs that are very close to work I've created, and I've learned to take it as a compliment, a sign that I'm evolving with the times. It happened with "Get Lucky," the Daft Punk song featuring Pharrell. I created a similar melody years before that one came out.

I wrote a song called "Trouble in Paradise" with one of Stevie Wonder's backup singers, and the next thing I know, Phil Collins released "Another Day in Paradise," again with the same melody. I'm not sure what happened there, but it was a strange coincidence.

Another benefit of being in Kool & the Gang is that we've worked with people like Marvin Gaye, James Brown, Sly Stone, Gladys Knight, the Temptations, and more amazing people. We were working in Paris at La Vénus Noire, and Lenny Kravitz dropped by and hung out. There were times that Stevie came and played with us. Back in the early days, he even sent a few bucks our way to keep us afloat. Also, it was an unbelievable compliment when the Godfather of Soul said that after himself, Kool & the Gang was the funkiest act in the world! When sampling gained popularity in rap and hip-hop, lo and behold, Brown jumped to the number-one spot as the most sampled artist, and Kool & the Gang the most sampled band.

I remember Ray Parker saying, "Remember when we all toured together and our bus broke down? Stevie made all of his band members get off their bus and he gave us his bus?" It's true that Stevie was very supportive of us, and I'm sure to many other Black artists trying to make it in this business. Our band took over Stevie's old business office at Twenty-Fourth Street and Fifth Avenue after he moved out. We always shared a close connection.

Charlie Collins was Stevie's tour manager and spokesman for quite some time. Back in the '70s, I stayed at Charlie's house when we were rehearsing in the area. I watched music shows like *Midnight Special*, studying groups like the Bee Gees to learn from their performances. Charlie would say, "What are you making all this noise for? I'm trying to sleep here. Go to bed. Stop listening to all that bumping and drumming." He was a bit older than us, and I remember thinking, *What's wrong with this guy? I'm just trying to have fun, man. Let's smoke some weed.*

He was something of a mentor, showing me how the business worked, but sometimes he liked to have fun too. I'd be back in Jersey, and he'd call from his office. "Hey, boy," he'd say, "get over here right now. I've got these two flight attendants, and we're going to have dinner." I'd go over and have a memorable evening with them. He was a wonderful man, just a wonderful person, and he still is today. In the downtimes he would call. "Hey, man. Everything's going to be good. You'll see." He was always supportive of my career. "Georgie should do this. He should be on this project." He was that guy, always.

The Collective Genius

When all our pistons were firing, when the band was in sync, there was nothing like it. Even when there were issues within the group, when we were in the groove, there was no denying the magic we created: "the collective genius of Kool & the Gang." When we were working on music, somebody would say, "Man, that is a special thing right there." Then we'd collectively focus on that piece of work and stay with it until it was just right.

Claydes was one of the writers on the Kool & the Gang song "Take My Heart," and the track is in 12/8. Each note gets a beat. The guys didn't like the track at first. I used to date a young lady who worked with Whitney Houston. I took the track and played it for her. Then I came up with some of the lyrics and took it to T.J./J.T. to see what he thought. J.T. said, "Hey, man, this is hot." The result was a number-five pop hit, but when it started out, people didn't like it too much. It just took time for it to grow into a Kool & the Gang song. It needed our collective genius.

I'm a lyricist as well as a musician. I come up with tracks too. When we were all in sync, Khalis developed the chorus sections, I dropped in the verses, J.T. tossed in a verse, and I worked with everyone on the production and harmonies. Then Kool weighed in with a different perspective. That was the collective.

For me it comes down to curiosity. That's what fuels me, but I've also learned the importance and power of humility. That can be difficult to remember when you're playing in a stadium in front of 150,000 people. It's easy to succumb to the rock-star lifestyle and the myth that you're invaluable, irreplaceable, and indestructible.

With age and experience come a more holistic view of the entire process, the phenomenon of celebrity and stardom. Over the years, I've learned to see it for what it is: a result of hard work and a lot of luck. That has allowed us to be successful musicians for decades. Now I make an effort to keep things in perspective and realize it's a true gift to be able to bring people so much joy. That's a great job to have, and plenty of other professions do that every day. No matter who you are or your station in life, it's about being true to yourself and your talent, doing what you enjoy, and following your own path. If you can positively impact others with your gift, that makes it all the more special. What I tell my children is to have faith in yourself, have faith in the Lord, and keep moving forward.

Anyone or any group of people can foster their own "collective genius." It's just a matter of believing in yourself and trusting those around you. When you do that, the result shows in your work. If I'm not moving forward, I'm not in step with the Lord. When I am in sync with my faith, that keeps me motivated. I take a step, and the Lord takes a step. That's my process. Others must find the path that works for them and their belief system.

Whether it's the Lord or another deity, I've found that it helps to have a spiritual support system, because it keeps me motivated, positive, and optimistic. So much happens in the mind and spirit before we begin to create. It's an attitude, a state of mind, a way of being and thinking. Pessimism only brings with it a sense of negativity and failure. The vibration of positivity is what carries me through the difficult times and allows me to fully appreciate the good times. You have to keep going no matter what.

Even when times are tough—and they are for all of us—we have to keep going. When we don't give up, we reach the other side and think, "Oh, my God, I'm so glad I kept going." You're rarely glad that you gave up, but almost always grateful that you stayed with something important to you. Through mindfulness and spiritual peace, I've learned to bless everything and truly appreciate the gifts I receive. Life is about adventure and exploring and learning and challenging yourself.

I've learned to move out of my comfort zone and challenge myself, both professionally and personally. I took flying lessons for a while as a personal challenge. Riding on those small private planes made me uneasy at first, but when I learned to fly, it gave me a sense of confidence, and I was able to fly solo my first year. *Yes!*

I did the same thing with martial arts. I'm a second-degree black belt, because I stuck with it and enjoyed the process, not just the result. The benefits were physical and spiritual growth. Plus, I can kick ass if it comes to that! Pursuing those interests and taking on those challenges helped me grow and gave me new experiences that help to inform my work and creativity. It's important that we open ourselves up to all that life has to offer.

I have to be honest that the main reason I do things like that is because I'm curious—or nosy, as my parents liked to say. I've always been that way. Maybe that's why people always told me I was "different." Going along with the status quo never satisfied me. My instincts have always been to find out more about something I'm interested in. Maybe it's my way of continuing to learn and grow. Sometimes, when we get older, we lose that drive to keep learning.

That's something I've tried to keep fresh and exciting. Learning and evolving help me to experience things in a new way, and it makes me feel—it doesn't matter whether it's happy, sad, anxious, or frustrated. I think it's important to keep challenging myself emotionally. Being a creative person, I must stay in touch with my emotions, because they directly affect my music and songwriting.

Possibly, that outlook is how I survived all those years in the public eye and traveling on buses, trains, cars, and planes to reach a venue in time to share my talent with the world. Then it was time to do it all over again. It's a tough life and a stressful life, no matter how lucrative it is. The same goes for working in the studio. It takes a lot of people to make things happen. There's no instant gratification of pushing the record button and creating a hit. So much goes into every project that it can be difficult to handle for people who aren't confident in themselves and their ability to create or bring out the creativity in others.

My mother used to call the entertainment industry the "heartbreak business." She knew that all too well because of the proliferation of struggling entertainers in our Jersey neighborhood. She knew how they worked countless hours for the opportunity to play music in a dingy nightclub in exchange for a few bucks, if they were lucky. She watched as many of them pursued dreams that never materialized. Maybe that's why it never felt intimidating or overwhelming for me. I was a kid with nothing to lose and everything to gain.

A Lesson in Creativity

The way I've survived the ups and downs of my career is that I've always had a strong belief in my God-given talents. We didn't have a lot of material wealth growing up, but I always felt the music inside me. It was always there. I thought about it, I dreamed about it, and I focused on it. Yet I learned early on that the key was to develop and nurture my creative nature to come up with work I could be proud of. It wasn't going to happen just because I had talent.

Surrounding myself with other talented, creative people helped push me to put forth my best efforts. You have to hold true to your passion and stay the course. You hear that so many times when people make their acceptance speech when receiving an Oscar or a Grammy.

"Believe in what you're doing, stay with it, and it will manifest." It's the truth!

Creativity is a skill that needs to be nurtured and inspired. Surrounding yourself with like-minded people and working at your craft will help to propel you forward. The caution is that the journey will probably be filled with detours and dead ends. It sounds cliché, but it's true, because it's all about how you handle the tough times.

That's why it's important to be as mentally and physically healthy as possible. Being creative can be exciting and fulfilling, but it can also be stressful. Frustrated musicians and other creatives can sabotage themselves if they aren't careful. Falling for the distractions, or my grandma's "devilment," not only can derail your dreams but can be dangerous.

The flip side is that when you've created something that brings people joy, you're raising the consciousness of humanity by entertaining people. There's a powerful satisfaction in watching people jump to their feet at the first few notes of a song you've written as they mouth the words that you poured your heart into creating. My mother also used to point out the other side of entertainment, the best side. If you get past the heartbreak, you are in the business of making people happy, and what could be better than that?

The human journey is a journey of unfolding experiences. Even when you come back here from other lives, you're unfolding, life unfolds, and creativity is the conduit for that. Being able to channel your creativity means bringing a new experience to your audience.

I always say, if life isn't a symphony, I don't know what is.

5

BRIDGE

―――――

WE PLAYED A SOLD-OUT SHOW at the Glastonbury Festival in London in 2011. Glastonbury is a huge festival that's been held for decades, and the lineup of artists is always an eclectic mix of fun. That year the festival included acts like U2, B.B. King, Beyoncé, CeeLo Green, Janelle Monáe, Radiohead, and Paul Simon. We had sixty thousand fans at our concert, and it was as amazing as you would expect.

After the show, David Lee Roth contacted the group. The rock band Van Halen was prepping for their 2012–2013 tour to support their new album *A Different Kind of Truth*. Roth was back with the band after a prolonged absence, and fans were excited to see the reunited group share the same stage once again.

Roth said he'd noticed our fan base at the festival was largely female, and he thought our party vibe would be a great addition to their tour. Anyone who looks at our catalog of music can see the diversity of genres and material, so we knew right away that it would be a good fit. Mixing rock with funk is always a good time, and that tour was no exception.

Kool & the Gang was able to open for several of their concerts before resuming our European tour. It was great fun for the Gang, because the music had to be pared down from the typical two-hour show to fifty hit-filled minutes. That meant a full-on musical assault of one hit after another to get the audience pumped for Van Halen. It was an unexpected double bill that surprised everyone, but I was having my own issues.

Being a vegetarian and focusing on my diet for so long often gave the impression that I was in top physical shape. That might have appeared true, since I watched my weight and worked out when I could, but I was letting small physical issues slip past while I kept my career as the priority.

While the Gang was having the time of their lives touring Europe and opening for rockers, I had to cut my part of the tour short to have stem cell surgery to heal a degenerative disc in my back brought about by the stress of many years of martial arts training. I'd put it off for way too many years. With a band as prolific as ours, there's always a reason to postpone personal obligations to answer the call of the music. That's what has kept the music alive for so long. The musical machine keeps chugging along.

It was tough to miss some of those history-making gigs, but it was time to put my health first. In fact, after that surgery, I began making time for other treatments aimed at helping me put more focus on my physical and mental well-being. An important tool that I added to my preventive health arsenal was vitamin drips administered through an IV. After the treatment, I feel an instant jolt, a vitamin-drip high that makes me feel like I can conquer the world.

One issue did pop up as a result of that decision. When the drip is taking place, I reach an almost meditative sense of peace and calm as I wait for it to run its course. After one such session, I found out a photo of me with an IV in my arm had circulated various social media outlets with the comment "Is George Brown of Kool & the

Gang feeling OK?" There I was with a needle in my arm and a dazed, euphoric look on my face. Of course, it was out of context, but still, it was not a good look.

I was so angry with the clinic for allowing such a personal, private moment to be captured and circulated on the Internet. After being in the public eye for so long, I've seen many scandals, but social media is a whole new world. Images and actions are easily misunderstood, and anyone with a keyboard has an opinion of what they think is happening, without any concern for the person in the photo. Incidents like that aren't just embarrassing; they can affect someone's personal and professional life if potential projects are shelved because of perceived issues. Unfortunately, it happens all the time, even if it's just a drip high.

Despite that mishap, having those treatments sent me down a path of trying other treatments designed to improve health and well-being. Out in California, it's common practice to experiment with the latest technology to achieve optimal health. I'm not a medical professional, so I can't speak to what anyone else should do, but these are some of the things I've tried on my health journey.

Ultraviolet blood irradiation requires that four large syringes be used to remove your blood into a 500-milligram bag. That is run through ultraviolet light to kill bacteria and other potentially harmful material in your bloodstream. UV light is also said to boost the immune system. I've been using that procedure for years because it makes me feel better, so it must be doing something right.

With another treatment I tried, a gentleman came to my house and took something like sixteen ounces of blood and put the hermetically sealed bottle into an ozone machine to infuse the blood. Then he put it back into my arm intravenously. The other option is to get the ozone in a saline solution that is administered using a drip.

One of the treatments uses what looks like a dialysis machine; they pull out the blood, and as it happens, you can see the clots and clusters make their way along the tube. Then they cleanse the blood and put it back into your system without the clots. The goal is to have healthy, clot-free blood pumping through your system to keep everything in working order.

I take a nicotinamide adenine dinucleotide (NAD+) every morning. It's a vitamin B derivative that is supposed to increase energy levels, improve mental health, promote sleep, improve memory, and even help fight aging. I usually take the capsule, but I've gotten the drip as well, and the "push," which is a machine that pushes it into the veins.

Like anything else, it has to be monitored, because too much can cause discomfort and even heat your body. It's like you're taking a shower, and the water is suddenly scalding—very powerful stuff.

I learned about herbs and the art of yoga from friends like Clifford Adams, a musician who has played in Kool & the Gang over the years. He was like a brother to me and helped answer some of my early questions about the best herbs to take or where to go for the best yoga classes.

My first wife called me one day long after we had divorced and said, "George, you were right."

That was a surprise in itself, so I said, "Oh, I was right about something?"

She said, "All those vitamins and herbs you got me to take, now my friends keep asking what I've been doing to keep looking so good."

It's not that I have any issue with traditional medicine. I've had procedures over the years to remove polyps or take care of other minor issues, but I hope preventive procedures will help me live longer and with a better quality of life.

I regret that I used to smoke cigarettes, which is probably no surprise since we played in many smoky clubs while we were coming up. It was much more common to smoke back then, and it was everywhere. There came a point when I realized I was doing it out of habit, and it wasn't making me feel good like it had at one time. I'm not sure why it happened, but it stopped being pleasurable, so I was able to quit.

Little Blue Devil

One issue I've always struggled with is sleep. I think it stems from those childhood dreams when I'd visualize the music and focus so hard on remembering every detail that it caused me to keep waking up. It was my way of visualizing my future, my goals. Somehow that might have morphed into an aversion to sleeping. I'm always concerned about improving myself and my craft, and sleep has, at times, seemed almost like a waste of time. There was so much I could be doing instead: working in the studio, going over songs, or searching for just the right keys, the perfect lyrics.

I stayed up for days at a time. My mind was just so active, constantly thinking, creating. I'd lose track of how many days I went without sleep. It was just a way of life. You'd be surprised by how much time you have when you don't sleep. I was in the studio for hours and hours. I watched TV or went for a drive, always looking for inspiration.

Finally, my wife said that I really needed to see my doctor. The first thing he did was prescribe Ambien. I'd heard the stories about sleepwalking, but that never happened to me, at least not that I know of! Ambien didn't do a lot for me. I was still awake. My doctor said, "Everyone responds differently to medications. Let's try something else." He prescribed Valium, so I was to combine the two.

"That seems to be a lot," I said.

"I have patients who take multiple pills," he responded.

Normally, I wouldn't do that, but I still wasn't sleeping. Two pills should be better than one, right? Then, when I saw my other doctor for an unrelated visit, he suggested Xanax. I was desperate, so I agreed. "Yeah, I'll try it." I knew other people who took them all the time, so I figured it would be OK. I didn't take them when I had a show, because I knew that was one area where I didn't need pharmaceutical help.

Once, we were traveling to a gig, and I was tapering off to get ready for the show; I could tell I was zoning out. Dee Tee (Dennis Thomas) came up to me and said, "Are you all right?" It made me realize that I was constantly high, even when I thought I wasn't. When I was awake, when I went to sleep, and when I woke up, it was just a constant fog of blissful indifference.

At one point, we were touring in Australia, and I was in my hotel room. My precious pills spilled on the floor. I tried to find them as they blended into the carpet, because I didn't want to run low. That's when it hit me that there I was, a grown-ass man, a successful musician, someone who's clearly had a blessed life, and I'm on my hands and knees digging my blue pills out of the carpet so I didn't have to go without them.

I had it in my mind that I needed to get help . . . when I got a chance. We were in another country getting ready for a show that had other big acts on the bill, including Lil Wayne. I knew I needed to be in good shape, so I went to the hospital because I didn't feel right. The doctor said, "You're probably dehydrated from those medications. You need to stay in the hospital." I called my road manager to let him know. They kept me in the hospital for four days. It was that bad.

The road manager said, "You can't continue onto the Japanese tour. It's too dangerous." After my hospital stay, I headed home to recuperate. I realized I was getting worse, and something needed to be done. This had been gradually building up for ten long years, slowly at first and then more frequently. I was at a crossroads. I needed help.

I called my brother in Maryland, because he works with addiction. His message was clear and to the point: "You need to go into rehab." I talked to my friend and adviser, Linda, to get another opinion. She had been sober for more than twenty-five years and told me to come see her. She performed a procedure and found that the ben-zodiazepines were detectable in my fatty tissue. "You have to check yourself in somewhere, George." I was all too familiar with the fact that going cold turkey can cause serious issues, including heart failure. Unfortunately, I've known many in the entertainment industry who have suffered similar issues.

When I checked into rehab, they took my blood and came back with a confirmation that my system was riddled with the effects of the combination of pills I'd taken for many years. I spent two weeks in the facility along with a roommate.

The doctor prescribed a high-grade form of Benadryl and other meds to help me sleep and wean me off the pills. That process was repeated every morning and every night to dry me out. They mixed elements of Alcoholics Anonymous and Narcotics Anonymous classes to help addicts change their behavior and mind-set. The AA classes were much more rigid, so I preferred the laid-back atmosphere of NA.

One night I sat up in bed and could feel my heart pounding against my chest. *Thump, thump, thump!* I thought, *Oh my god! What's happening to me?* I put my feet up against the wall to steady myself until it calmed down a bit. Then I made my way to the dispensary downstairs and told them what was happening.

"We expected this," the attendant said. "It's part of the process. You are now going through withdrawal." It was three days of intense sweating, shaking, and tolerating chills that coursed through my body as it adjusted to life without artificial stimulants pumping through my veins. Once the drugs were completely out of my system, they said, "Now, this is the psychological part you must deal with, George."

In my drug-induced thinking, my plan was to detox and then rejoin the Van Halen tour while working on the psychological part. After I checked out of the facility, I was ready to get back to work. I flew to Fort Lauderdale for the next concert, and the car picked me up at the airport. I was so discombobulated that I didn't know how to use my cell phone. My brain was on the fritz after rehab. I was in a strange mental space.

I was able to do sound check and play the gig. Afterward, I was lying in bed thinking, *Oh no, I'm having trouble falling asleep! Here we go again!* A fellow musician on the tour named Mike gave me some advice. "Go buy some regular Benadryl," he said. I had to take about four of them, but it worked. I made it through the rest of the tour, but I kept thinking about the psychological aspect. I still needed to work on that part, probably for the rest of my life.

Songwriters Hall of Fame

I was fortunate in that after my two-week stint at the rehab center, I was able to continue my therapy and resume working with the band. I've been able to stay off the pills since then, but I remain aware of any prescriptions my doctors suggest. Once you're an addict, it doesn't just go away, but I'm determined to never let that happen again. Being sober makes the good moments in life so much more important and impactful. That's what happened when we were awarded an incredible honor in 2018.

That's when four Kool & the Gang members—Robert and Ronald Bell, James "J.T." Taylor, and I—were inducted into the Songwriters Hall of Fame. That was such an especially important recognition for me as a songwriter and creator. Others inducted that year were John Mellencamp, Alan Jackson, Allee Willis, and Jermaine Dupri. Mariah Carey even showed up to support her friend Jermaine. I was surprised to learn that the Songwriters Hall of Fame has been around since 1969, started by the great Johnny Mercer, among others.

Plenty of big shots in the music business attended our ceremony, along with countless popular recording artists and musicians. It was one big party, and it made me think back to that ambitious group of teenagers who asked a church pastor if we could use the basement to practice our music. That was our launching pad, and we never stopped. How many folks can say that? People rarely start something at such a young age and have it last a lifetime. That's the part that always blows my mind.

Naturally, we had to perform "Celebration" that night to commemorate the event. It felt great to have the band back together with J.T. at the helm, even if it was just temporary. It had been about twenty-five years since he left, and despite everything, that night was about the music, and it was magical.

I always say that those songs are like our children. We nurture them, we put our heart and soul into them, and they are with us for the rest of our lives. They are part of us. It was nothing short of amazing to have our peers honor us for those amazing songs.

The Lonely Truth

Why are musicians and other people in show business in relationship after relationship, and then when they're on the road, they need somebody? A Bobby Womack song called "If You Think You're Lonely Now" talks about that paradox. He says his woman complains that he's never home, then when he is home, she complains that he isn't making any money. That's the story with entertainers. I don't care who it is. Touring is a solid way to make a steady income, but it takes a toll on relationships.

When you're home, it's all about the problems—the kids, the house, the appointments. Then you go on the road, because that's your livelihood, and the problem is that you're always gone. Throughout time musicians have written songs about the trials and tribulations of life on the road, and it's easy to brush that off as "first-world problems," but it's all in how you look at it. It's similar to over-the-road drivers, people working on an oil rig, or any profession that requires you to leave home for days at a time to make a good, honest living.

I've talked to fellow musicians about it, and there's a phenomenon that occurs where at first you feel lonely on the road and can't wait to get home. Then it morphs into feeling lonely on the road and lonely at home, because once you are in town for a while, everyone is going about their own lives, following the paths they've carved out while you were away. You're expected to keep yourself busy without having cultivated a routine at home. So there are times when you feel less lonely back on the road, where people understand you. It's a ridiculously vicious cycle.

I spoke with a friend about it, and he said, "There's nobody to talk to. You can't talk to your kids because they don't want to hear it from their old man. They aren't as excited about your latest award or a song you're sure will be a hit. That's just not on their radar, and the older ones already know everything. They've heard the industry stories. You can't talk to your other half because they think you're talking about yourself too much, and you're already a self-centered artist. You can't talk to friends who aren't showbiz people because they can't relate, and they also think you're talking about yourself too much. Nobody's listening."

When I first made some money, it felt so rewarding to help out my family financially. I gave my mom the money that allowed her to buy a house in 1978. I got a condo for my sister, and I gave my brother a down payment for his house. But I learned to be careful with money when it comes to family. It's sad to say, but it can cause trouble. Someone might think they didn't get as much as someone else, and it spirals from there. I have to walk a fine line with the people who were once my support system and most vocal cheerleaders.

I've never gotten used to the loneliness. I've been very personable all my life. I like to hang out with people and explore a new city or see the sights. I even like going to clubs when I'm in the mood for a party. I remember once, when the band was going to the club, my manager at the time said, "Hey, man, we're trying to get these girls.

I'm not into hanging out with a bunch of dudes." I didn't realize the trip was just about scoring with the ladies. I was just enjoying the atmosphere, meeting new people, and listening to new music; I came to find out they had a different kind of fun on their mind. It's not that I had an issue with that, but I was married and not interested.

I've met plenty of women over the years on the road, but rarely because I was on the hunt for company. It's happened more organically, by meeting someone and feeling a connection. I've never been the guy who heads to the clubs to find some action. It's fine for those who want to do that; it just wasn't me.

I remember being on an elevator in Holland, and there was this gorgeous girl, mixed Black and Dutch. We had an instant attraction. We were drawn to each other, and just as we were about to kiss, the elevator door opened, and we started laughing. I've always found that having an attraction is a prerequisite for me, regardless of background or status.

I'm not sure why I've dated so many international women, those of different races, backgrounds, and religions. What attracts me is, of course, physical appearance, but also intelligence, honesty, a sense of humor, and independence. Women who are originally from different countries seem to have a much different outlook on life than those I've met in the United States. My first wife was a Black girl I met in high school. I hadn't gained a lot of relationship experience at that point, but I held on to the idealized notion that we would navigate the uncertain future together. It worked until it didn't.

Even though I've been through it, the effects of divorce never diminish. The pain might fade into the subconscious ether, but it undoubtedly rushes to the cranial forefront at the smallest trigger. Knowing that it's usually for the best doesn't lessen the immediate or long-term effects, but we soldier on. That's the key to life, isn't it? Take the bad with the good and keep it pushing. "Do your best." That's all we can ask of ourselves.

My first wife was everything I was looking for—attractive, driven, and independent. She went to college and eventually became a high school principal. She was also a Jehovah's Witness. I was so proud of her accomplishments, and I never wanted to overshadow anyone else's dreams. I think having our own careers gives us purpose, focus, and pride. However, our divorce wasn't as easy as I wish it could have been. We separated in 1978, and we each retained counsel to hash out a settlement in the sterile courthouse, surrounded by practical wall paneling and utilitarian office chairs. Huddled pairs scurried past me in the hallways as they whispered back and forth.

Because we shared two children, ours was a bit more complicated, but naturally, my commitment was to provide for my boys. Once the financial aspects were settled, we enjoyed a respectful relationship as she raised the boys and I spent time with them between tours, but there were occasional issues that could only happen to someone in my position. Once, I received a letter because she was upset that I didn't mention our sons in my thank-you speech at an awards show. (My two sons from that marriage are stable, mature men who have gone on to have their own jobs and families.)

While many of my romantic interactions were just for one night, I've remained friends with several of my former girlfriends. A very important one is from Indonesia. The first time I went to Australia, I was dating a girl from India who was drop-dead gorgeous. She wore her hair in a short pageboy style that was sexy as hell. She cut it like that as a celebration of her heritage. I'm a chocolate guy; she was even a bit darker than me, with Asian features. My first time in Ghana resulted in meeting someone, but not the African girl I'd expected. She turned out to be Japanese.

One day I was leaving the New York Kool & the Gang office and waiting for the elevator. A woman came out of nowhere and said, "George, let's go fuck." I've had many romantic rendezvous, but when a woman is so forward, it never fails to catch me off guard. She was a lovely girl from England. She was an au pair who had just broken up with Stevie Wonder's brother. We had a relationship for quite a while.

Then I ended up dating one of Stevie's backup singers. She was a creative writer and talented singer who had attended Berklee School of Music. She was a Black woman, and we collaborated because of our shared love of music. We wrote some songs for a film project and found out we had distinctive creative approaches. My way is to write the music out in long form.

She said, "I don't work like that."

I said, "Well, in Kool & the Gang, we do that periodically."

"That's not the right way to do it." She was a sister with opinions, which I respected.

So there's not a shortage of people to meet, but for me, the loneliness never completely goes away. It's almost embarrassing to talk about, because I've had so many blessings that if loneliness is the price I have to pay, then so be it. It's just a difficult situation to be in, no matter where you go or whom you spend time with. Any reprieve from those feelings of isolation is only temporary. I'll feel good for a while, like I'm really making a connection and being understood, and then it's time for the next show.

Folks on the outside only see the two hours of performance, the meet-and-greets, the photos, and the autographs. There's so much more that goes on, and that time spent in public can be fulfilling, but the attention is no substitute for genuine companionship. Just like a lot of entertainers often say, it's lonely at the top. Most people can't relate. People want to know about the band, about you; they want details. I always told my wife, "Don't tell anybody where we live or used to live. We can't do that. It can get out of hand."

The odd thing is that the loneliness follows me. It finds me when I'm on the road, and it's the same at home because no one understands what it's like. They don't want to talk about the show or the things I've seen. It's old news for them. If I talk about the people I met, they think I'm bragging or just focusing on myself. In reality I'm just trying to share my work and my interests with my family.

Trying to find someone who just wants to talk and have an enjoyable evening can be an effort in futility, because it seems like everyone wants something. They want more from a relationship; honest friendship isn't enough. Sometimes, I could easily tell the groupies from the women who were genuinely interested in me, but it could be difficult. Being married has never had any effect on the number of aggressive ladies who approach me. The words *I'm married* fall on deaf ears when you're on the road.

Fidelity can also be a slippery concept for both parties. At one point I had a condo in a nice building in Los Angeles, and I allowed the woman I was dating to stay there as my guest. There was this wonderful African American surgeon who also lived there, and we were friendly with each other. One day I ran into him in the restaurant attached to the building, and he blurted out, "Hey, George, I'm not screwing your old lady."

We all know what that means. I said, "OK, well, thanks for telling me you're not, but you're a busy man. How would you have time for that anyway? You've got patients to tend to."

I knew it was true and was torn up about it. I talked to my mom for some solid advice. She said, "Just because he said he's not going over there doesn't mean he's not going."

My brother chimed in as well. "She's gorgeous. Any more of them around? You got any more of them?"

I said, "You can take a shot. I'll step back. I don't want any part of that."

Later I confronted her in the apartment. I didn't mention my run-in with the doctor. I just went up to her, knelt on one knee, and cleared my throat. She looked down at me and batted those long lashes like a coquettish deer as she smiled at me.

I took her hand in mine and said, "Could you leave me, please?"

She was silent for a moment, and once she'd regained her composure, she said, "I'm not going anywhere. Can I get some money?"

What the hell? I was friendly with her parents, so I gave them a call and told them what had happened.

The mother said, "Well, you've got to give her something. It's only right."

I responded, "No."

Next I called my attorney, who said, "I knew she was a slimeball when she first came up here. You were so in love with her, and we thought you knew she was gaming you."

So as the natural course of action, she dragged me to court in an attempt at a shakedown, alleging that we were in a committed relationship and were supposed to get married. I went to the courthouse to give a deposition, and I saw her sitting outside the room chewing on gum, as usual. I was pissed that I had to be there, but I couldn't deny that she was gorgeous!

I came out once I'd finished. She was still there, working on her gum. "George, you know I still love you." *Sigh.*

One thing I learned is that most women do not handle rejection very well, at least in my experience. I was romancing one woman, and all of a sudden, she was on the bed and ready for action. I came close to doing the deed, but it was just such a turnoff that I stopped and said, "This doesn't feel right. Let's just say goodnight."

She was not happy. "Well, you've already got it out, you may as well put it in."

That was even less attractive.

The Black Stones

After we paid our dues on those dusty U.S. backroads on bouncy old buses, we enjoyed the upgrades that success afforded us. Being able to fly made travel much more convenient and the trips quicker. Those are some of the perks that come with being in a successful band for several decades. Not only that, but our venues naturally got larger as we were able to fill them with eager fans.

We have also built an especially fervent fan base overseas and spend a lot of time playing concerts in other countries. Concert requests are usually for festivals, private shows, and even luxurious weddings.

We did a show in France that a father provided for his bride. He owned the largest vineyard in the country and had ties to the oil industry in the Middle East. He was flying us there to perform for the special event. Imagine being able to have the actual band play the party songs everyone wants to hear—"Ladies' Night," "Too Hot," "Joanna," and of course "Celebration." At that event they even had bedazzled porta-potties spread out on the grounds, complete with twinkling lights and custom paint jobs to match the theme.

For another wedding, we were flown to Egypt and discovered two Gulfstreams waiting to transport us to an area near the Libyan border. That's where you see those pickup trucks full of guys in the back with guns pointed in the air. We were in the middle of the desert preparing for a show put on by the biggest resort owner in Egypt. It took place at one of his beautiful venues, but it started raining—in the desert! We only played for seventeen minutes, but everyone seemed happy, and we stayed to socialize.

I'm very spiritual, and I think that's partly because I have those visions of dancing lights and vivid dreams that often come true. Once, I was in a mild state of slumber when one of those visions appeared. That time, it was the Virgin Mary. After that vision, I went to Berlin and met a buddy who lives there. He's from Egypt and was adopted by a German couple. When we first met, he thought I was Egyptian, and we struck up a friendship.

"Are you sure that you aren't Egyptian, George?" he asked.

I laughed. "No, I'm from Jersey City."

"Well, you look Egyptian," he insisted.

Curious, I had my DNA tested to analyze my genetics. I discovered that my parents' lineage could be traced back to ancient Egypt, so maybe my friend was right after all.

While I was in town, I visited my usual massage therapist, who takes care of many musicians. She's amazing, and she said to me, "Tell your friend he's not going to die." I thought she was probably talking about one of our road managers, who was diagnosed with cancer, but that seemed to be in remission, so I wasn't sure if that was it.

She continued, "I understand that you're going to Paris."

I said, "Yes, I am."

Then she gave me some water.

"What is this?" I asked.

"It's water from Lourdes, France. I want you to go to the Chapel of Our Lady of the Miraculous Medal in Paris, France. It's where the Blessed Virgin Mary appeared to Saint Catherine Labouré in 1830."

I said, "Yes, I know. I wear my own miraculous medal, and I just recently had a vision about the Virgin Mary."

She smiled, "I want you to go there, and I'm going to give you the name of a young man: Swinn. Say a prayer for Swinn. Write it down, and then give it to the nuns there."

Before I could go to Paris, we had a show to play. Each year, the royal family of Bavaria, Germany sponsors a show for the residents of the town of Regensburg. So the band was there to perform and socialize with our hostess and her family. The crown princess came up to me and complimented the medal I wore around my neck. I said, "That's the cathedral, the chapel of Catherine Labouré, on Rue du Bac, in Paris."

She said, "Yes, I know. I go there when I can. My daughter has a medal as well."

We played a show in Austria, home to the Habsburg dynasty. The Habsburgs don't enjoy any political power but remain a fixture in

Austria. I was approached by Francesca von Habsburg-Lothringen's aide, who said her highness was a big fan of the band. She often traveled on her yacht to see us perform in nearby cities when we were in the area.

She said, "George, Francesca wants to see you on the yacht."

"I would love to, but I have a sore throat. I don't think it would be a good idea."

"Oh, please do come," she said. "Please?"

"Seriously, I'm not feeling well, and we are leaving in the morning anyway."

"We have plenty of food. You'll feel better."

"I am hungry, but I'm a vegan."

"Then you must come. The chef will prepare anything you'd like. It's settled."

Once I made it to the yacht, I sat down to observe what was happening. Almost immediately, Francesca slid into the seat beside me. "I understand you have a sore throat."

"Yes, I'm afraid I do," I told her.

She asked someone to retrieve her purse. She reached in and brought out an atomizer. "Open up, George."

"What is—"

"Just open."

Then she gave me a couple of sprits of the elixir. I'm thinking, *This is European royalty, a dynasty I learned about in high school, and she's spraying my throat.*

Then she instructed her assistant, "Please get my beads that came from the Dalai Lama. I want to give them to George."

Someone came back and said, "We can't find them, your highness."

She seemed agitated, so I said, "The reason they can't find them is because they're meant for you, Francesca. The Dalai Lama gave them to you. Most likely, you'll find them after I leave the yacht."

"That's possible," she said. "Right here I have a shirt that was given to me by the people of Tibet. It has my likeness in the form of a deity with zirconia stars on it. Please take this as my gift."

Rubbing elbows with people like that still amazes me, because I find them so fascinating, and yet they are telling me how much our music has impacted them. The first time Kool & the Gang played in Monte Carlo, Prince Albert, Liza Minelli, and Princess Stephanie showed up. I always play those shows the same, but I can't forget the important people out in the audience. It still astounds me.

We've done concerts out in St. Moritz, up in the Alps of Switzerland. St. Moritz is a luxury town where the Olympics have been held twice. It's just breathtaking, and it should be when the elevation is almost six thousand feet.

At the other extreme, we were in Saudi Arabia at the request of a prince. He put together a concert with his favorite performers, so we were on the bill with Julio Iglesias, Andrea Bocelli, Lionel Richie, and Sister Sledge.

I stayed in the city of Medina, a holy city and site of a major Islamic pilgrimage. While there, I visited the Al-Masjid an-Nabawi, also called the Prophet's Mosque. It was simply gorgeous. The concert was to be held in the nearby city of Al 'Uyūn, which was actually in the middle of the Arabian Desert. Some of the performers were flying there, but because we stayed in a nearby city, a driver was assigned to get us to the venue.

Somehow our driver got lost in the desert. It got dark, and we were soon driving through miles and miles of an endless desert at night. It was eerie. I'm sure it was to distract me, but my English chaperone began talking about the amenities in the desert and said there are five Michelin-star restaurants in the vicinity of the concert. I don't think there are even five restaurants in Los Angeles with that rating. I said, "In the middle of the desert?"

He said, "Yes. People who live here, who frequent them, know where to go."

We continued driving, and at one point, nature sounded her inevitable alarm. I said, "Is there any way we can stop for just a moment?"

"Oh, no, we don't do *that* in the desert. We'll be there soon."

"But we're lost," I said.

The driver seemed offended. "We are not lost!"

I can tell you that we were indeed lost. So I said, "Just pull over. I'm sure Al-Qaeda does *that* in the desert, and so does ISIS. Can we just stop?"

Thankfully, they agreed, and we pulled over. I got out and called the road manager. "Man, we're lost in the desert. I'm with an Arabian guy, a Caucasian woman, and then there's me, a tall Black guy from Jersey. I'm not sure what's going on, but I know we are lost, and I don't want any trouble." Fortunately, luck was on our side, and we made the concert just in time, but I was a nervous wreck. I hate that helpless feeling that can sometimes come with travel.

This was nothing like Dubai. We'd played there before it was so built up and then again after. In the beginning, all the streets were still sand. There were a lot of condos and office buildings. I stayed at the Hilton on Jumeirah Beach. I was in the hotel eating my vegan meal, and I saw an Arab gentleman. He had on all the regalia, with a drink in one hand and a cigarette in the other.

Over the speakers, I heard my friend Lionel Richie and the Commodores singing "Easy." I looked over and the gentleman was rocking to the song, just swaying in his seat. I thought, *Look at that. We're in Dubai. He's got on his traditional garb and rocking to Lionel Richie.*

It goes to prove the age-old adage that music transcends everything. People are people, and we experience similar emotions. We are one. It makes me wonder how any of us can harbor negativity or even lash out at each other merely because of race or appearance. If you see people from all over the world and their common denominators, the things that affect all of us, like music, the idea of racism seems ridiculous. We're all so much more similar than we are different. It just feels like many people don't want to accept that fact.

That concept is never clearer than during our concerts. With our extensive catalog of songs from various genres, we get a true cross-section of society: young and old, all races, and all economic levels. It has become almost a generational tradition, where parents and grandparents will bring their children and introduce them to the songs they grew up on. It's like the Rolling Stones, another band that just keeps on going, bringing together a wide variety of people. It's all about the exuberance and party atmosphere. People are dancing and singing along. How can there be any animosity? Music fosters just the opposite: love and unity.

We have been dubbed the Black Stones, because like the Rolling Stones, we tend to hop all over the world without slowing down. One show is in India, then Sri Lanka, Macau, Hong Kong, and Singapore. There's no favoritism with us. We enjoy playing for everyone, regardless of where they are. We even play countries like Romania, Poland, and Slovakia as well as cities like Frankfurt, St. Petersburg, and Moscow. It just amazes me that a band of Black men plays these countries and sells them out.

It's truly about the music, all over the world.

The Performance

Tours are a busy time for us, because the schedule is tightly booked to take full advantage of our time on the road. It's usually four days on and three days off. That can last for a few months, and then there's a break. I used one of our breaks for my rehab stint, because I hoped that once I was clean, I could get back on the road, where I feel most comfortable. Fortunately, it worked out.

When I'm home, it's gotten to the point where I will just stand by the window inside my studio and watch everyone go about their day. That's especially true if my kids are upset about something or I feel especially lonely and, frankly, unappreciated. What I do for a living isn't seen as exciting or special anymore. It's expected. Business as usual. Sometimes, I just hang around the house in comfortable clothes and try to keep myself occupied until touring begins again.

That's one of the reasons why I started studying classical piano. It was a new challenge, something familiar but not comfortable.

Then I talked to my former teacher and said, "I want to get back to the jazz stage."

He said, "I'll find you a teacher."

I said, "My classical piano teacher is great, but I want to get back to jazz." I enjoyed learning the classical style, but that's not my passion. Jazz is what we started out playing years ago, and that remains my true musical love.

Now I'm back into learning more jazz, new techniques, just to get back to familiar territory. It's like a muscle that hasn't been used in a while. You have to put in the work to hone the skills. Those activities help keep me occupied and challenged until the next tour comes up. When that happens, I have to prepare myself, physically and mentally, for the challenges of being on the road. It's certainly rewarding, but sleeping in a different place most nights (even if it's "luxury") can be a grind, and navigating the travel challenges is another obstacle, especially since we primarily fly these days, which can be unpredictable. One of the aspects of the tour that I especially enjoy is the camaraderie with the guys in the band—the familiar, easy banter. I also like meeting new people, and part of the job is hosting meet-and-greets and talking with fans.

When I was home, I tried to educate my two sons who live with me on how important it is to cherish what we have and be appreciative of our good fortune. As we drove around Los Angeles, I'd point out a building. "You see these people who don't live in big homes with all the toys? They don't have a pool of their own, they don't have a gym in their house. Your life is much different, but it's important to realize that most people don't have what you do, so we have to be humble and grateful."

Los Angeles has such a problem with its homeless population, so I'd bring that up and compare it to their situation. However, as young men, they didn't seem to understand the depth of what I was trying to tell them. "Just look at everything around you," I'd say. Their response was usually "Yes, Dad, can we go home now?" Then they would hop into the Audi S3 or the BMW M2, and away they would go to hang with their similarly privileged friends.

Recently, we were having work done on our house, another privilege we enjoy, and I asked one of the boys to help me with one of the projects. "I'm doing something" was his response, and it set me off. Just because we have professionals running the construction doesn't mean we can't pitch in.

Raising children is tough, and raising young Black men is a whole different challenge, but I've found that raising them in a wealthy area like Los Angeles, where it's about what everyone has, requires a different set of parenting skills. Of course, most of their friends are in a similar situation, and it is human nature to compare circumstances. The hottest cars, the latest Rolex, the trendiest restaurants—it's endless.

I'm sure we all try to get our children to understand how good they have it, but it doesn't seem to resonate with my boys. When I was coming up, we didn't have a lot and I knew it, but I didn't feel deprived. I was appreciative of the things we had. Maybe I'm more aware of our circumstances because I made many sacrifices to get here.

I might also see things differently because of the constant touring. On the road, I see all types of people from all walks of life. It's a sobering reminder to appreciate what we have, because so many are going through tough times, especially in countries where financial inequality is even more evident.

These days our tours follow a similar pattern. First I get a call from the tour coordinator. "Hey, George, how are you doing?"

"I'm doing fine."

"Well, OK, the car will be there at 5:45 AM tomorrow to take you to the airport. You're getting on JAL, Japanese Airlines, and the flight is at 11:45 AM, nonstop to Narita Airport."

Then someone texts or emails the itinerary to make sure I have everything I need. It's usually a black SUV that picks me up in the morning and promptly drops me off at LAX. Sometimes, a greeter is waiting for me and gets everything situated and sends me to the lounge to relax before the flight.

When it's time, I board the plane, and it never fails. As soon as I sit down and get comfortable, our tour coordinator calls. "Are you on the flight? Is everything good?"

"Yes, I'm on the flight. All good."

"Now, when you land there'll be a gentleman waiting to pick you up. He might be holding up a sign. At least he should be."

Once I land, another call comes through. "Are you with the driver?"

"Yes, I'm with the driver."

"Great!"

Then the road manager—who is already in town—calls: "Hi, GB. You in the car? I'll be waiting outside for you."

The car pulls up to the hotel, and here comes the tour manager with a big smile. He settles up with the driver as the hotel valet takes care of the luggage.

I'm led to the suite, and the valet goes through the checklist of how things work and the amenities available on the property. Once he leaves, you can guess what happens.

The phone rings. "Are you situated? Can you come to sound check?"

"Yes, I'm a little tired, but I'll be there."

"Great. Security will be at your door at 8 PM to escort you. Can you be ready?"

"Yes," I assure him. I've only been doing this since I was a teenager. Granted, the circumstances have changed drastically since the days of smoky lounges and shifty nightclub owners who may or may not pay up at the end of the night.

Soon enough, there's a knock at the door. "This is pickup."

"I'll be right out," I respond.

They escort me down the back elevator and say, "Have a good show tonight. I know you guys are going to burn it up. I've always been a fan, and my wife loves you. Could I get an autograph?" Then we walk down the long hall to my dressing room.

Once the show is over, there is an explosion of people backstage. Excited fans still buzzing from the show mill around all over the place trying to locate the band members. Sometimes we do a meet-and-greet and line up to talk to fans, take photos, and sign something for them.

Then the road manager says, "Security is here to take you back to your room." That breaks up the crowd, and people move out of the way. Back in the old days, we might have had help from the local police department to get us through the crowd, especially if we were in New York and it was dangerously crowded. They would even check our rooms before we entered to make sure no overly enthusiastic fans were crouched behind a piece of furniture or curled up in the closet.

We usually have a floor reserved, because we have a large crew, and it means no one else should be there unless they are a guest of ours. We used to play football in the long hallways to blow off steam after the show. Back in the room, I invariably get a call from an industrious young lady who somehow found out which room I was in, or maybe she called them all. I don't know.

"Hi, I'm Candy. I'm downstairs. Can I come up and say hi?"

The next morning, we put our bags outside the door to be collected and routed to the next location. The road manager calls and says, "Mr. Brown, your car is downstairs." Sometimes, a few of us pile in, since we are all going to the airport. We talk about the show and, more important, what happened after. Back in the day, there were some wild stories to share.

Then we get to the airport, and if we're going out of the country, we stay on the plane while everyone else exits. They take us off the side of the plane and put us in a car on the tarmac. We go to a special lounge that's unoccupied, and they bring out the food we've requested. They take our passports and submit them to security, where they are stamped. Then we're ready to go. There's no checking our bags or anything like that.

If we fly privately, the captain says, "Let me see your passport. OK, you're fine." Once we land, especially if it's a Middle Eastern country, someone will pick us up with security and drive with a steely determination to our hotel.

Once, we were playing on a bill with the rock group Cheap Trick. The plane was late arriving in New Orleans, and when we finally landed, the greeter took us to the Mercedes van, and the state troopers escorted us through the unrelenting rain. They blocked off freeway ramps and side streets to get us to the venue as quickly as possible. They even brought our stage costumes to the van so we could quickly change before we were ushered to the stage. Those frenzied moments get me pumped up for the show, but they can also be a bit disorienting.

Sometimes, the disorientation is my own doing. Once, in Greece, I was drinking ouzo and it got the better of me. I was stumbling through the street with money spilling out of my pocket, and it started to rain. I finally made it back to the hotel, but I felt horrible, clogged up with sinus and cold issues. I had trouble catching my breath, and that's when I swore off alcohol.

But before that, in the '80s, we played the largest soccer stadium in Kuala Lumpur, Malaysia. Apparently, we broke the ticket-sales record previously held by James Brown and the Rolling Stones, and that's why people started calling us the Black Stones. After that show, a guy approached me and said, "Hey, George: you, me, and all these girls at my place."

I was a single man at the time and up for some fun, so I said, "Sure."

We hopped in the nearby cars and arrived at his place. It was just a bunch of women and two guys. I had the time of my life. So much so that when I returned to my hotel room, one of the crew members was already packing my clothes, because we were heading to the airport to make our flight to the show in the Philippines. There I was, smelling of alcohol and, uh, companionship, and maybe a touch of marijuana.

In Bordeaux, France, we exited the plane and, once we got to the street, saw one of our guys already there and with a woman. One of us said, "What are you doing? We've got the show coming up soon!"

One time I had a scare when I thought I had contracted gonorrhea. I talked to a local doctor, who assured me, "Mr. Brown, you will be fine. Just be safe from now on." Fortunately, I didn't have an STD, but it did freak me out for a bit.

As a young man with money and fame, it can be easy to fall for life's temptations, like when I was physically held down by two women while they took care of their own sexual needs. All I did was provide the equipment and see it through to the end. I'm guessing that's why entertainers and celebrities are so well versed in attorneys and divorces. It's practically an occupational hazard.

At some point, it becomes a lifestyle. A lot of situations are destined to escalate. They are initially well intentioned, but alcohol and libido are a tricky combination. In Judaism they say you can't put matches and wood together, because you're going to make a fire. For us, a rock 'n' roll blaze burned almost every night.

Plenty of times, we smoked marijuana in the plane bathrooms. The flight attendant put a blanket over our head, turned on the air suction, and closed the door. We blew the smoke right into the exhaust.

I did that on a trip to Düsseldorf, Germany, and dumped the seeds and residue in my carry-on. I approached the immigration and customs station, and I was able to pass through with no problem. But one of the valets behind me had a pipe clipped to his belt for some reason. The guards herded us all back to the station. They went through all our bags, even squeezing the toothpaste out of the tubes, breaking bars of soap in half, and shaking out our clothes. At one point they gave my carry-on a nice shake, and out came the seeds and residue I'd hastily tossed in. I used to keep them in the cuff of my jeans, but not that time.

They asked where we were going, and someone said Berlin. So they called ahead to our hotel in Berlin and found out a friend had brought marijuana there in anticipation of our arrival. Upon discovering the contraband, hotel security had asked our friend where he got it, and as he told us later, he looked at them and said, "Harlem." Then he told them the whole story: "All I gotta do is go down to the Jamaican health food store on 148th Street and get my shit." He was right. Sometimes, when we landed in New York, anyone into coke went to a house in Harlem to stock up, and I went to the health food store for some marijuana. Anyway, we all got detained, but we were soon allowed to resume the tour. Our friend in Berlin also escaped unscathed.

We were in Frankfurt one time and feeling particularly, uh, randy. We were all looking for some companionship. So the road manager arranged for buses for the band and crew to drive all of us to a cathouse.

Anytime we went to a strip club, once the strippers realized who we were, they left their other clients and spent all their time with us. That didn't make us popular among the other guys in the club, but that was just fine with us.

Tour Mishaps

We've had some crazy mishaps onstage. After "Too Hot" had just been released, we were playing the song at an outdoor show on a scorching afternoon. Someone yelled, "Fire!" We looked over, and somehow the piano had burst into flames! We finished the song, and the audience was none the wiser. Just part of the show. I like to think it was because our newest single was burning up the charts!

Fans can get a bit overzealous. Many of them would jump onstage and grab us or attempt an awkward hug or kiss before security ushered them to the side and out the back door. Some just wanted to do a little bump and grind in front of the audience, but security was always watching.

We were touring on a double bill with Earth, Wind & Fire when they had the amazing Al McKay playing guitar. Anyway, they stayed to play on the peninsula of Italy, and we went to the nearby island of Sardinia. We were performing for an exclusive crowd of important, obviously very wealthy people. We finished the show, and one of the band members stayed behind to talk with some of the beautiful ladies, because they were always the first ones to rush up after the show.

Same thing happens in Monte Carlo. We often play at a sporting club there where the tickets are $1,000 a pop, and it's always an honor to work on a stage that has been graced by performers like Frank Sinatra and Whitney Houston. After the show, we typically go to a nearby club called Jimmy'z because it's where all the luminaries migrate for late-night revelry and devilment.

So we were in Sardinia, and while my buddy was conducting his own meet-and-greet after the show, a burly gentleman approached him and said, "Sir, my boss loves the band."

"Oh, that's great," my friend said, "thank you so much." Then he returned his attention to the attentive ladies.

"Sir, my boss would like to have you come over and talk with him about the music."

"OK, OK, I'll give him five minutes."

Then out of nowhere, he gets slapped so hard he tumbles over the table he was leaning on.

The burly man said, "You disrespect our boss?"

We soon found out "the boss" was the son of a well-known dictator, and he was obviously used to getting his way. Some of our crew members were told that we would never be able to play in the area again. It was unsettling for us, and we wasted no time flying back to Italy and meeting up with Earth, Wind & Fire to tell them about our run-in.

We have gone to Chile several times to play at the Viña del Mar International Song Festival. It's a huge Latin musical extravaganza, and the stage reminds me of something out of Cirque du Soleil. The festival started back in 1960, and it's the largest in Latin America. Along with the artists who perform, there's a singing competition, a beauty contest, and a raucous audience made up of people from all over the world.

On one occasion, we arrived early and gathered outside of the hotel, where we were met by a journalist and camera crew. As we were being interviewed, thousands of fans had gathered around, eager to see the performers arrive. The crowd became a bit unpredictable, so we were put into a van and taken to a nearby mall to spend some time until the crowd dissipated.

Naturally, we headed to the music store to look at the latest releases. As we were sifting through some great music, we were recognized, and fans came toward us from seemingly out of the woodwork. They were everywhere, and it was apparent that they were excited to see us. We were led out the back exit and ushered into the awaiting van.

One of the guys in our crew met a Chilean girl, and I'll admit she was gorgeous. He brought her back to the hotel, and we all made it through the gauntlet of fans and press. One of the hotel staff stopped him and said, "Sir, please don't bring any guests." This guy gets agitated and says in a loud voice, "Do you know who I am? I'm with Kool & the Gang!" The journalists in attendance pricked up their ears, and cameras swung in his direction. On the local news, the story got twisted, and they proclaimed that someone from Kool & the Gang was taking a minor into the hotel.

During the Gulf War, we were touring in Algeria, of all places. The country had wonderful international hotels, such as Sheratons and Hiltons, which I find are much more ornate and luxurious outside the United States. They are five star, and these days, those are the hotels I like to stay in, if possible. I've paid my dues in plenty of low-budget motels during my career.

We were in this gorgeous hotel, and we were advised as Americans to stay on the property, which was fine by me. At one point, we got to the airport to board Khalifa Airways. I took a couple of photos in the airport and was quickly surrounded by military soldiers. One of them said, "Give me the camera. No taking pictures at the airport here in Algiers." *OK, whatever you say.* So we flew into a beautiful city located in the desert of southern Algeria. This time the hotel we were taken to was one of the filthiest places I've ever seen, and I've seen lots of them.

I got to my room, and the carpet was dotted with at least a thousand cigarette burns. I would have played connect the dots if it hadn't been so nasty. There were two outdated speakers installed on either side of the bed, a touch screen, and thick cobwebs decorating each of the corners. One of the other guys said he had a dead pigeon on his balcony, but fortunately, I did not. The hotel did provide robes as an "amenity," but I chose not to wear the one provided. Instead, I met the guys downstairs to eat. Some of the others are vegan as well, so we look for similar food choices.

We ended up with French fries, and some of the guys ordered chicken. It was covered with a spicy green sauce that also had some extra protein in the form of flies. Not only that, but some of the little pests were also still flapping their little wings in an attempt to escape the goo. One of the guys sent it back and asked that the flies be removed. Because of the language barrier, it was returned with a larger portion, still topped with the innocent insects.

We felt it was safer to spend our time at the bar. One of the crew stayed there all night. When we got back to the room, a local Arabian band was practicing in the next room as we tried to sleep in anticipation of the show the next day. The melodic modal sound wasn't bad; it was just poorly timed, because we were trying to rest up for our performance. It's no wonder I suffer from insomnia.

The next day, we were driven to the venue, an old colosseum located in the center of the ancient Roman city. It was a beautiful reminder of the area's rich history and instantly made me forget the dodgy hotel experience—well, almost. The colosseum was doused in twinkling lights that accented the stoic columns that rose out of the desert floor. The concert was sold out, with around thirty-five thousand people attending, and the show was nothing short of magical—an amazing experience.

After our performance, we were assigned armored military vehicles to escort us out of the venue, because the war was still going on. We traveled through several little cities on our way back to the hotel. I was drinking a lot of water, because my throat was dry after the show. Maybe I consumed too much, because I really had to make a pit stop. I asked the driver if we could find a bathroom. "No, no, no," he adamantly replied as we creeped slowly through the arid desert.

I really had to stop, so I asked our road manager what to do. "George," he said, "just open the door and do your thing while we drive. Problem solved." Frankly, I didn't have many options, so I headed to the back of the van. The driver pulled the van to the side of the road and stopped abruptly. "Go!" he shouted.

Gingerly, I stepped out into the sand, which was still hot despite it being pitch black aside from the military spotlights guiding us to civilization. One of the military vehicles swung a giant spotlight on me so that I could make sure there were no snakes around. I appreciated the gesture, but I didn't want to be on display. I waved at them and said, "No, it's OK! No light!" They were unmoved, so I did what I had to do while illuminated by a piercing white light. I saw it as my own encore after such an amazing show.

Recently, we were in Dubai, a place we travel to often for gigs. Of course, our crew had several different food preferences, but we were sure they could be accommodated. At a restaurant, one guy asked, "Can you get any pork?"

The waiter whispered, "Of course. I'm Filipino. How much do you want?" We learned that pork is taboo in many Arab nations based on Islamic law. It felt almost like a drug deal to have to order pork secretly. Would we have to meet them in an alley to make the transaction in the safety of shadows?

One of the stark, bitter realities that always leaves an imprint on my mind is the extreme poverty in places like India. We were staying in a beautiful hotel that had guards outside the gates. It was a stunning place, and that only served to accentuate the extreme deprivation that we saw while driving around the city. I looked down the side streets and saw hundreds of disheveled people, many with no shoes, huddled under makeshift tents in an effort to escape the merciless sun. There were kids giving directions in exchange for spare change. I'd see small children walking by themselves and wonder what their story was. Where were their parents? Were the children safe? Would they make it home? Then we would play our show, and the concert was always sold out. It's the haves and the have-nots, to the extreme.

That's Dope

One vice that has helped me throughout the years is marijuana. I've been smoking or otherwise ingesting it since the '80s, and it does serve to ease many of the issues I've suffered from, including depression, anxiety, and insomnia. It isn't foolproof, but it works more often than not. Now that CBD is legal at the state level in California, it's much easier to find exactly what I need.

I usually get straight THC, and it never bothers me. I guess I've built up a tolerance due to my decades-long usage. Back in the '80s, I was practically a Rastafarian and smoked just about everywhere I went. Now there are so many options, such as edibles, tinctures, creams, and on and on.

Not long ago, I got a THC tincture to try out and took two and a half droppers full. Then I had a nice meal that my wife had made. She treated me to many of my vegan favorites—spinach, corn, potatoes, and roasted garlic. After eating, I was full and happy, so I got ready to Netflix and chill.

A couple of hours later, something didn't feel right. The high kept getting bigger and bigger. I thought I'd experienced it all, but nothing like this. The typical arc was that the high took over, lasted a while, and then subsided, allowing me to drift into effortless slumber. This time it plateaued and then got higher with no warning. It freaked me out, because it was so unusual. I seriously thought I was dying. I even tried praying for it to subside, but it continued to get worse.

My wife came to help and asked what happened. I told her I'd taken about 2,500 milligrams and something wasn't right. She looked at the bottle and said I was supposed to take 0.25 milligrams, not 2,500! Apparently, when trying a new THC delivery method, it's best to go slowly and add to it gradually, but as a seasoned pro, I didn't think that was necessary. Man, was I wrong.

I said to my wife, "Please call 911, because I'm about to die. I don't know where I'm at. I don't know what to do." I was inside my body but outside my body at the same time. It felt like I was taking a mushroom trip, which I've never done, but that was the only thing I could compare it to.

Back in my partying days, at the height of the '80s, there were people who would deliver whatever we wanted to a rehearsal studio or writing session. We were young and invincible, so I thought I could handle just about any type of marijuana. Back then I'd also chase it with lots of cognac. That was my jam, marijuana and cognac, and then I was good to go.

As we were waiting for the EMTs to arrive, my wife tried to calm me, and I tried to find my inner peace. I worked hard to focus on what was happening to my body. I kept telling myself that I needed to maintain focus and not let this THC control me. I could hear myself saying, "Yes. OK. I'm good." I was trying to convince myself, but I knew that I was not good at all. I was a mess.

The other side of me was saying, *No, you can't, because you're outside this thing and you're not getting back in there.* I repeated, "You got to call 911, honey, because I took—"

"Yes, I know, George. You told me that you took too much, remember?"

The EMTs finally arrived, and I heard one of them talking to me. It was almost like they were talking underwater, their voices muffled but finally coming in clear. "Are you high, sir?"

I said, "I think I took too much THC. It was an overdose." It felt strange to say that, because I never even thought it was possible to OD on marijuana, but that's what it felt like.

They checked my heart rate and declared that everything seemed fine—elevated but not dangerous. "Sir, you seem to be in great shape. Your blood pressure is up, but that's about it."

I said, "Yes, I know it's high anyway."

One of them said, "What would you like to do? Do you want to go to the hospital?"

At first I did, but then I realized there was probably no need. Now that I logically understood what had happened, the only real option was to wait it out until the high came down.

"Are you sure? It looks like you took two and a half doses of the thousand-milligram dropper."

Live and learn.

A Lesson in Well-Being

Somehow, by God's will, I survived the rambunctious lifestyle the music industry practically demanded of me, and I happily complied. I lived the rockstar life and took full advantage of the perks that came from the hours and hours of practice, hard work, and hustling. I was fortunate that I came out of it reasonably unscathed.

Through it all, I learned a lot about others, but I also learned so much about myself. That life tested me in ways I could never have imagined. Just like anything else, some days were amazing, and others were heartbreaking. That's life, isn't it? It's not so much about the good and the bad, but instead what we do with those times and what we learn from them.

Do we strive to improve ourselves? Do we try to change the things we don't like and celebrate the things we do? That's what I take away from my life as a musician. How can I make things better for me and those around me? How can I show gratitude for all my blessings while honoring my hard work and talent?

In the beginning, the madness and mayhem were exciting, a thrill I knew was reserved for a sacred few, the highs of performing onstage, of hearing people shout your name, of watching throngs of sweaty, smiling fans moving their bodies and singing the words to your songs. Sometimes it astounded me that the words they sang so effortlessly were the same words I'd pored over, agonized over, trying to find just the right flow and rhythm.

As I looked out into the crowd and saw them embracing our songs, I had to remind myself that I had put so much effort into those lyrics, so much love. I always strive to get it just the way I hear it in my head. That doesn't always work; in fact, it rarely does. I think it's almost impossible to replicate what I hear and feel in my dreams, but I do my best to try and shape the message into a song that will resonate with our audience.

That might mean it is delivered with an irresistible hook or a seductive bass line, but it's the words that people relate to, that make them feel. Being able to make people smile or laugh or just feel good is a reward that is beyond description. As a musician and a songwriter, the goal is to reach people in their soul and spirit. When they hear a song that's important to them, it brings back memories, the good times, or maybe the sad times. Either way, it makes them feel something, and that's an amazing gift to be able to share with the world.

But I could never have gone for so long in this industry and reached so many people without also taking into account my well-being. Musical history is filled with tortured artists who literally and figuratively died for their craft and often left an indelible mark on many people, but then it was over. To me, being able to ride out a career that spans decades and continue to innovate and grow is where we can make the most impact and affect the most change.

My philosophy has always been to follow my intuition and chart my path, even if it went against the norm or didn't fit the rock 'n' roll stereotype. It's always been important to take care of my physical and mental state, and that allows me to keep going and keep giving the best way I know how: through music.

It hasn't been an easy path, but few are, and putting in the work is what makes it so rewarding. Having an outlet for innate creativity is truly a gift and one not everyone is given, so I've always tried to honor that.

If we stay present and learn about ourselves every day, as musicians and creative people, we can pour those lessons and emotions into our work. And if we get it just right, we can craft a message that reaches others and plays an important role in their lives.

As artists and as humans, it's up to us to find effective ways to use our talents to create an impact. It may be joyful, melancholy, or even sad, but the goal is to find the emotional center and deliver it in an impactful way.

I could never have imagined that my musical dreams as a young boy would lead to so many experiences and opportunities. And every one of those helped to inform and educate me so that I could put that in my music.

Learning how to take care of my physical and emotional needs in a healthy and sustainable way over the years has allowed me to continue honing my craft, because it means I am not burdened by self-inflicted health issues or crippling mental battles. I've had plenty of stumbles along the way, and there are things I could have done differently, but we all go through that.

What it boils down to is that taking care of ourselves must be priority number one, because only then can we care for others. As artists, when we make solid personal decisions, it means we can focus on our craft and give it the dedication and respect it deserves.

When experienced entertainers can share and mentor and teach newer artists, it completes the cycle. The ultimate gift is to share those valuable lessons with others so they can learn what works and what doesn't. Then they can take that information, allow it to inform their creativity, and hopefully avoid some of the pitfalls others endured.

Whatever your craft, whatever your niche, whatever your skills, become the best you can be. You might be an accountant, an attorney, or a teacher—delve into it and study as much as you can, get as much information and education in what you're doing as you can, and keep an open mind.

Everything is not going to go exactly the way we want it to go. Yet when you're passionate about something, it's up to you to move forward and go for it.

There's a Japanese saying that is something like "Keep your chin strapped tight," because there will always be challenges. When there's no war, there's going to be war. When there's war, you know there's eventually going to be peace. What I always urge everyone to do is pray, meditate, hold yourself in high esteem, and make sure to stay positive. Misery loves company, and idle hands are the devil's workshop. Keep yourself occupied. Do the work. Occupy your mind. Continue to educate yourself.

If you're a painter, and you paint well, go paint more. Bring that out. Whatever you're going through, bring that out in your painting. If you're a songwriter, if you're an actor, if you're a carpenter, go to work. Make something happen. Bring something alive. Develop something.

If you're prone to negative thoughts, do something to keep your mind busy. That helps avoid the "woe is me" scenario that is easy to fall into. Say to yourself, "How do I construct this? How can I make this better?" That's the mind talking. *So, George, how do we construct this?* And I say, "You know, mind, I don't know. What do you think?" The mind says, *You know, I think . . .* That's our internal dialogue, our way of finding solutions.

When you have downtimes, remember that we are all living on this rotating blue ball of life, and we all go through difficulties. I don't care who you are, how rich you are, how gorgeous, you're going to go through something. For me, the only way to go through it is to pray, meditate, and hold yourself in high esteem. You owe yourself that much.

Get out in nature. You don't have to hike unless you like hiking. Do what you enjoy, just change the environment, shake things up. Look at the beauty. When I mentor artists, I encourage them to see things differently. Say you're driving down a city street. Don't allow yourself to be distracted. Stay focused and pay attention to your surroundings. What do you see? Traffic, architecture, people on the sidewalks. Imagine what it took to create that. Now think about the people walking by and what they might be going through that day.

Look at the Jewish deli, Chinese restaurant, or corner dry cleaner. Those businesses might be minority owned or female owned. They all have their own stories, and the people had a dream to open those businesses—even the guy on the corner with a food cart. They've all made choices, and that's part of their dream. It might be the final step or just the beginning. That's up to them to decide, but they have brought it to fruition.

The tire store I go to opened in 1956. It was started by a man named Hank who is no longer with us. He was the soul of that business, and he and his family treated everyone like they were important. After all, they were. They still know most of their customers by name and ask them how things are going. They are invested in their clientele.

People are drawn to the business because their passion is evident. They are experts at what they do, and it shows. All of this, all that we do here on this planet, comes down to hopes and dreams and the ability to bring them alive.

I read a book about up-and-coming bands, and some make it clear that they are not interested in fame. Their focus is to develop a modest but supportive following that allows them to play gigs and earn a decent living. They don't model their career path on someone else's success. That's a smart way to move. Measuring your success against others almost always leads to disappointment because you're seeing it from the outside. You have no idea the struggles they've endured, the hardships, the sacrifices. And you might not be willing to make those same choices. It's about finding your way.

6

OUTRO

THERE'S NO DOUBT that I've been fortunate to channel my talent into a career that has lasted since the late '60s. Not only that, but I've also reached professional goals that I never even imagined when I started out. My focus all along has been to make a living playing good music that people enjoy.

My career with the band hasn't always been easy, but it has been fulfilling and has provided me with many opportunities. I've been all over the world many times. I've met celebrities, politicians, and royalty. Now my priorities have shifted. That's not to say I'm not still driven, but I've done many things I set out to do, and that allows me to focus on other things, such as my family, health, and solo projects.

Just to Make Her Happy

I've put a lot of work into creating a stable family environment, before and after I had children. As far as relationships go, I was at heart always a one-woman kind of guy. Sure, I've had tons of fun on the road as a single man with plenty of opportunities for female companionship, but my preference has always been a committed relationship. That journey has not been an easy one. However, I've remained focused on finding the right one for me, as evidenced by my marriages. Even though some of them didn't last, I never swore off the institution. I never gave up.

I have learned along the way that it takes a special person to hitch her wagon to my star. I'm a creative musician, a driven entertainer, and a perfectionist. It can be difficult to be with a person in this industry, not only because of the obvious temptations but also because of the demands of the job. Being on the road, spending hours and hours in the studio, strategizing with my team—it's not a traditional life, and many folks don't understand that until they are in it. It seems bright and shiny on the outside, but the reality is often much different.

I've found that some women are initially intrigued by the idea of being with a celebrity. Then when it comes down to daily life, it can mess with a person's head. Some feel lonely when I'm on the road for months. Others can't get past the jealousy as I interact with fans or work with up-and-coming female artists. I've learned that no matter how much I reassure them of my devotion, the doubts usually linger. Some can handle that, most cannot.

I met my current wife through a gentleman who was a biochemist. He said to me, "George, I hear that you're doing a show." We were playing an exclusive show for Ferrari owners, and tickets were difficult to obtain for anyone else. He said, "I have a friend and she'd like to go, but I heard that it's a private show."

"Yes," I said, "but I have two tickets you can have."

That night, I looked for my friend, but he wasn't there. He had given the tickets to his friend, who it turns out was a Chinese woman I had previously dated. She brought along a friend who was Vietnamese.

"It's good to see you, George," she said. "I know you didn't expect to see me."

"I didn't, but I'm glad you're here."

"I'd like to introduce you to my friend. Her name is Hahn."

When I first met Hahn, she was graduating from college and knew little about popular music. She'd never heard of Kool & the Gang. She had dark, beautiful hair that cascaded down her back. I was stunned by her unmistakable beauty. I invited them to dinner at a hotel on Vine. We were on the top floor overlooking the twinkling lights of Los Angeles, and it was an amazing night.

Later I asked Hahn for a date, but she was in San Francisco for a while. It took a few weeks before she was able to return to L.A. When she did, I invited her to a restaurant on Wilshire Boulevard in Beverly Hills. It was a hot spot for actors, musicians, and others in the industry. I was used to going there after shows, because most clubs in town close at 2 AM, when a musician's night is just beginning.

We had a wonderful evening. Our conversation flowed effortlessly, and I was entranced by her exotic looks and undeniable intelligence, the quality that never fails to get my attention. Intelligence lasts beyond physical attraction. For me, it's what takes a relationship from lust to love. We had an amazing night that lasted until early the next morning. I found out that she had grown up in Long Beach, near the Vietnamese community in the Westminster area of Orange County. After that, our courtship picked up steam, and we were exclusively dating for months, even taking lavish trips to tropical locales like the Bahamas. We finally got married in 2000.

She is a gerontologist and has two eldercare businesses in California, one in Orange County and the other in Mission Bay. She has a thriving career that keeps her busy, and she has no interest in show business. We talk shop sometimes and give each other advice, but other than that, we stay in our professional lanes.

She is a Vietnamese woman from Japan, and marrying someone from Japan has been a cultural adjustment. My wife's a princess from a wealthy family. While we dated, I loved learning about her culture. When I first met her relatives, her grandfather shared some sake and said, "Welcome to the family." Her parents were born during World War II, and her father was in the kimono business. They had a beautiful traditional Japanese-style home in Tokyo and another in a remote location where hot mineral waters helped them grow orange trees. They were a very entrepreneurial family, and I loved the drive to create a better life.

We have two boys, and after all these years, I've learned many things about how to get along with an Asian woman like my wife. She is a perfectionist and likes things a certain way. If she gets upset, she becomes quite vocal, which caught me by surprise at first. She is not shy about voicing her displeasure at something the boys or I am doing. For example, Jordan doesn't eat on a regular schedule. He has an unconventional appetite, like his dad. I always say, "Eat when you're hungry." I don't like to allow the clock to dictate mealtimes. To me, that is unnatural and unhealthy. I try to listen to my body and focus on what I need and when I need it. My son follows a similar anti-schedule, and it frustrates my wife, because she's the exact opposite, a stickler for time and schedule.

Once, before we were married, I was late for a party, and she raised hell with me for days because I had arrived late. It's not out of malice or ill will. She said it's because of her culture, which is steeped in the concept of respect. For her, everything is about honor. If I'm late or not hungry at mealtime, she sees it as a sign of disrespect. I've shared with her that it's not the same for me. I follow a more peaceful, serene type of thinking. I tell her, "To get peace, you've got to be peace." She agrees, but lifelong habits are hard to break. If we need some space, I retreat to my studio, where I can lose myself in the beauty of music, while she reorganizes the house to her heart's content.

I've been through a few marriages, so I'm determined to see this one through, but of course, no relationship is without challenges. It takes work. She's focused on being perfect and following a regimen at home and in her business. That's why she is so successful and can run two clinics. It's a monumental task, and she's phenomenal at it. We are each successful in our chosen fields, and I often have to remind myself that just because we see things differently doesn't mean one of us is right and the other wrong.

After COVID, our lives changed considerably, as did everyone else's. We had to let go of the people who helped around the house, so my wife took on all those responsibilities along with her work in health care. She also follows her cultural tradition of shopping daily for fresh produce for dinner. Her mother is the same way. When her parents visit, her mother stays with us, and her father goes to a hotel to keep out of the way.

Education has been a priority with my family. My oldest, Dorian, went to Norfolk State and studied communications and computer science. Now he produces hip-hop music and has his own thriving business as a licensed exterminator.

Jorge graduated early from high school and went to the New Jersey Institute of Technology, Rutgers University, and DeVry University. He has worked as a computer designer in the medical industry and with NASA, and now focuses on cybersecurity.

My second wife convinced our only child, Gregory, to attend college in Japan, where she said there were "proper schools." He went to the Aoba-Japan International School and graduated from Temple University in Tokyo with a degree in business. He was in the music group New Classics and is a songwriter, producer, singer, and rapper. Today Gregory lives in Japan and is a well-known pop star signed with Crown Records.

I like that we share a love of music and Japanese culture. The people there are so polite and courteous, and the streets are immaculate, which I love. They emphasize cleanliness, with bath time being an important part of the day. Maybe that's why their stress levels are noticeably lower than in the United States.

My two youngest still live at home. Jordan, nineteen, is a brilliant student and is studying engineering. Aaron, seventeen, is an accomplished pianist and also plays drums. He's planning to major in business. I applaud all my sons in their endeavors, and I'm so happy they are successful in their own right. They have created their professional paths, and I couldn't have asked for anything more. I joke with my wife and say that I'm so happy we didn't end up with any knuckleheads.

I've always been curious about my culture and heritage. I had my DNA analyzed, and the results were interesting. I am 2 percent Thai and 2 percent Myanmarese, and I even have some Chinese in me. There's also Spanish and Portuguese. A woman texted me from out of nowhere and said, "We share the same Chinese grandmother from two hundred years ago."

One of the times that we went to Africa, one of the band members was excited because he was Nigerian. He eagerly greeted a man on the street with "Hey, brother!" The Nigerian was not amused. "I'm not your brother. You're an American Black man."

The first time I went to Ghana, I was so happy because I was the first in my family to touch these shores where we supposedly had a genetic connection. I met a guy named Jamal, and we quickly became friends. He said, "I'm pure African, George. You, my brother, are a half-breed."

I said, "Oh, thank you."

He added, "I'm Muslim. That is a Black man's religion. You should be Muslim. You're a half-breed while I'm pure African."

"OK, I got it. Now, try to get a visa to the U.S.," I joked.

I shared my bloodline with my brother and all my sons to show that we descended from a tribal bloodline. Our lineage can be traced back to Ramses III from Egypt. Apparently, 55 percent of African American men have the same lineage, just like 40 percent of Chinese men descend from the first emperor of China, Qin Shi Huang.

My father's side of the family migrated from Egypt to West Africa, where Sierra Leone, Ghana, Nigeria, and Mali made up one country until the colonists came along and declared, "This is for France!" and "That is for Spain!" My mother's side also came from Egypt and migrated to Mozambique, in southern Africa. I like to think that might be why I have such a love of travel. My goal is to visit every country that makes up my lineage.

I think for Black people here in the Americas or people in Europe who are of African descent, we're all so mixed with European ancestry that it's rare anyone is a "pure" race. All populations are made up of a complicated history of mixing and migrating around the world.

W. E. B. Du Bois wrote that the biological concept of race categorizes people based on physical attributes and commonalities, while the sociohistorical concept of race refers to shared group experiences. He thought that viewing race that way was more accurate. His point was that physical traits (blood, color, and so on) are not the only qualifiers of race. He theorized that in the twentieth century, there are no races in the pure sense, just groups of people with shared experiences.

I can relate to that, because based on my experiences around the world, my involvement with women of many races, and the results of my lineage, it seems that we all have more in common than we have differences. I think the Black and Brown cultures contribute to our country's rich tapestry. If we all traced our lineage, I think we'd be surprised at how the similarities link us. Maybe it's naive, but I see our culture as stronger when we come together instead of being divisive.

It's Part of Me

My music teacher gave me a wonderful compliment. She said, "George, I want to tell you it's a treat and a joy to work with you. You're such a gifted musician. As a teacher, you just give me joy working with you."

I just looked back at her and said, "The music is just part of me. It's an amazing thing."

Even though I've had decades of success, it excites me when someone talks about my musicianship. For so long the accolades and focus were on the success of the band and the big hits. Often, people don't see the talent and skill that goes into that success. Of course, not every gifted musician is blessed to make music all their lives, but some are, and it's because of hard work and innate talent that can't be phoned in. It takes a lot of work and commitment. Kool & the Gang put in the work—all of us—and we always have.

The magic happens when a band can make the music look effortless. Onstage we are smiling and dancing and harmonizing, and we're clearly having fun. It's a party! Yet a lot goes into that production, including years of devotion to the craft. It's not only that but also the dedication to following those dreams and not giving up. Our band was not always at the top of the charts. We had our ups and downs, which is part of the game, but we kept at it. When our first song was on the radio, we thought we'd made it, but it was really just the beginning. We showed what we could do, then we had to back it up. We had to keep going despite financial issues, management problems, or interpersonal relationships. All of that is just noise when you look back. Keeping the music alive and entertaining our fans is always priority number one.

Industry people frequently drop by my studio to check out what I'm working on or to discuss a potential project. Recently, the head of Universal Music Publishing Group paid me a visit and listened to the solo music I've been working on. He's a classical pianist, and after he heard my stuff, he was quiet for a moment and then said, "George, you have timeless ballads and some slamming tracks. How can we help you at Universal?"

Do you know how that makes an artist feel? The head of Warner Chappell Music (now president of Sony Music Publishing) also visited me. He did the same thing: listened to my new tracks, paused for a moment, and said, "We'd like to offer you a publishing deal, because the music is amazing."

I've also been in discussions with a film producer to provide the music for the soundtrack to a couple movie projects about famous musicians. I would be providing source music, or underscoring, to be used throughout the movie. The gentleman listened to some of my songs and said, "I've got to work with you, brother. I've got to work with you. Based on what I'm hearing, we need to work together."

My business and trade partner said he wasn't surprised by the reactions I've been receiving. "Man, your musical sensitivities are wide. Whatever the type of music, you can make it happen. If somebody says, 'I need a classical piece,' you knock it out for them. 'Some innovative jazz?' No problem. That's not something a lot of musicians can do."

Do you get my point? A buddy came by, and I played a piece for him called "Dreamland in Sleepy Town." He listened intently and said, "That's you on a piano playing, right?"

"Yes," I said. "That's what it calls for, some piano."

It's a strange phenomenon, because it's like something just takes over, and I get into a creative groove that feels so natural and so right. Time becomes meaningless, and my only focus is on making good music. That's the gift that I accepted all those years ago. I've nourished it, developed it, cherished it, and embraced it. Music has been such a blessing to me, and a creative outlet that I don't think I could live without. It fills me with such joy when I create a song that resonates with people. It excites me every time it happens.

A buddy of mine helped pull together a small orchestra to work on some music and see what we could create. I had a song called "One Bed, Two Dreams," and I got an idea. I had a feeling that it should be done in Italian. That just felt right for the song, but then we added an orchestra behind it at a certain point in the song. The title refers to a couple in a bed, and both people are dreaming about what love should be: one bed, two dreams.

A great composer and conductor friend of mine called and said, "Man, come down here. Let's do this. Let's make some music." I get those requests from a lot of folks, but for me to be creative, it has to be the right time and the right feeling. One day I was talking to him, and the phone connection wasn't great. "Where are you?" I asked.

"George, I'm just getting on a plane to Tehran. I am now the conductor of the Tehran Symphony Orchestra."

Having friends and contacts in the industry from all over the world is still a trip for me. Growing up poor and Black, we didn't have the opportunities that a lot of people had. We didn't meet people like that. If we wanted to make things happen, we had to figure it out ourselves.

Khalis used to say, "Stay the course if you're passionate about something—really, truly passionate." My mother had similar advice. "If you truly want to be a musician or whatever it is, stay with it. Work for it, and it will come to fruition. You are what you think. Whatever you think about the most, that's what you'll become."

They were both right. I'm a born drummer. It was easy for me, so I started coming up with different patterns and calling them "Funky George," because nobody was playing those types of flip patterns. It turned out to be super innovative, and everybody else started doing it. Then when sampling came in, all the rappers started sampling me. I became the most sampled drummer in the world. That still blows my mind. Then Kool & the Gang became the most sampled band.

All those rhythms—that's me. Do you hear all those beats in rap songs? That's me. They either sampled me or they copied. People ask me, "How did you come up with that?" I'm just doing like Ronnie used to say: "Khalis, he's playing himself." I'm just playing me. I'm doing what I feel is in me. That's it. People said, "But nobody has ever played anything like that before." To me, it just came naturally, not because I was trying to do something different.

Ronald and I did an interview in England years ago because we had written a lot of the songs. He said, "You know you wrote the song 'Sugar,' George?"

I said, "Yes."

He said, "That was long before Barry White. He copied your style. When you listen to his song, you can hear the piano changes."

I said, "Oh my God. That's true."

He had a point I hadn't considered before. Barry White popularized the sound that I'd created, because I wasn't as skilled on piano, and it just came out that way. I'm a better piano player now, but back then I was just doing what felt natural. I tried other instruments, like guitar and blues harp, with similar success.

It's gratifying. It's beautiful, and I'm thankful and happy. When I hear one of our songs on the radio, sometimes I take it as an omen. Something could go down, and I'll turn on the radio, and there's a Kool & the Gang song playing. I'll turn it up and think, *I'm in total gratitude. Love and great gratitude to everyone who loves the music and helped us along our way.*

There's no word to describe it. It's like, *What a blessing.* You pray to the Creator, the Musician. What can you say? You say, "Thank you, and thank you, and thank you" to exalt the Creator.

Ronald and Robert Bell could get totally absorbed into the music. We all had such a pure love for the craft. There's been talk about remixing some of the hits, but I think those are sacred to us. You don't see Marvin Gaye's music being redone. "Hey, let's remake 'Can I Get a Witness' with a song contest winner." It doesn't work.

With music consumers and their ever-changing interests, it's tempting to try and rework a song to make it more marketable to a different generation, one that doesn't necessarily want to listen to their parents' music. Yet so often when that is done, the integrity is lost, because the melodic integrity, the magic of early collaborations, can't be recreated.

Astana

I started the Astana Music Group to create music for myself and others who represent my point of view and display my talents. I came up with the name when I was in Monte Carlo for a gig. I kept seeing commercials for a city in Kazakhstan called Astana, which is now known as Nur-Sultan. It was touted as a shiny new metropolis where everyone was welcome. I liked the idea of a place that was so open and willing to embrace people from all walks of life, much like I've always done.

My goal from the beginning was to create a record and production company that would initially focus on dance and pop releases. It didn't take long before I'd signed six artists to the label. It's no surprise that they were a diverse group.

The roster has a distinctly international flavor (my specialty), with Chelsea, who was born in the Philippines; Dominique, a Canadian American; Jonna Elizabeth, from Denmark; Chiyumba, from Kenya; Jordan, from Israel; and Mychelle Nychole, from the United States. My label also has a stable of songwriters, sound engineers, producers, singers, and musicians such as the acclaimed talents Keri Lewis, Leon Silvers, and Rick Marcel.

The first release from the company was an infectious 2018 dance club track called "King Size," fronted by the sultry power vocals of Chelsea. We worked hard on that track, with me producing and cowriting. The talented producer Alessandro Calemme and his DJ team created four remixes and the original radio edit.

Next we released a single that we wrote as an empowering anthem for women all over the world. The message of "Pink Tool Box" is to embrace your strengths and not worry about what other people think. The song begins with Chelsea repeating the song title to the sound of a strumming guitar and a smooth, dreamy groove. Over the synth-heavy production, the song has a minimal yet flowing groove, complete with a cadence that complements the lyrics and a collab with New York rapper NexXthursday, who provides a fresh vibe as the composition changes to a classic hip-hop groove. The single has been remixed by several famous DJs, and the video was directed by ZANE, a visionary who has worked with people like the Isley Brothers, Afrojack, and David Guetta. The song was a dance smash, especially in the UK where dance music thrives.

Chelsea has been in the Top 40 several times, and her social media presence is on fire. Her video for "Pink Tool Box" has more than a million views, and her song "King Size" has more than 2.1 million. She has around half a million followers on Instagram. She has impressed me with not only her natural talent but also her dedication to her craft and the business, because it is, first and foremost, a business. It's not all red carpets and autographs. Many artists don't realize the work and sacrifice that is required, but Chelsea has been determined to make her mark in the industry and has the results to prove it. It has been rewarding to see headlines like CHELSEA DEBUTS ON BILLBOARD DANCE CHART WITH "PINK TOOL BOX," and CHELSEA'S "PINK TOOL BOX" JUMPS TO #33 ON BILLBOARD DANCE.

Jazi was born Marisa Sundari Freed to an Indonesian mother and Caucasian-Jewish father. After she broke onto the Hawaii hip-hop scene, she created a buzz throughout the industry. She became the first Hawaiian hip-hop artist to be featured on outlets like *World-starHipHop*, *XXL*, and DatPiff. She was also nominated for Hip-Hop Album of the Year for the Na Hoku Hanohano Awards in 2014. Once she came to Los Angeles, she released a mixtape called *Talk to the Mic Volume 2* that garnered a flood of attention and excitement. She has even created an organization, Little Girl, Big Dreams, to inspire women into leading and living better lives. I was excited to sign her

in 2019, and she became Jzi Muzic. Her songs include "Forever" featuring Niki FM, "It Don't Matter," "Don't Get Mad," "Take Off," and
"Glue (Stuck with Me)."

Jonna grew up in Copenhagen and was influenced vocally by
Whitney and Sade. She has developed a unique, soulful vocal style and
has been performing throughout Europe, from Demark to Germany
to the French Riviera. Her debut song, "I Come Alive," debuted at
number thirty-one on the UK club charts and has continued to grow.
The video has a fun party vibe that even pays tribute to the old-school
Soul Train line dance as Jonna warns listeners, "I come alive."

For years I've known Maria Papapetros, a psychic and healer
who is famous worldwide for her perceptive abilities. She was born
on the isle of Crete in Greece, with a father who was a healer and
two psychic aunts. She has worked with many in the entertainment
industry and even government agencies, bringing a new language of
self-actualization that elevates a healing process to an art form and
the field of psychic development to a science. I worked with her on
a project when I brought in actress/singer Vanessa Williams, whom
I'd met in Tokyo when she was crowned Miss America.

Because Astana is my baby, I am smart enough to bring in the
right people to help make things happen. On video shoots, I love
being part of the energy and watching the action, but I let the professionals do their thing. I might give some suggestions here and there,
because it's a collaborative effort, after all. Sometimes, I bring in a
female director from Gilboa, New York. She has such an artistic eye
and provides a different vibe. Her work goes beyond music videos and
into film and old-school moviemaking. Astana takes a lot of energy
and effort, but it's creative, fun, and fulfilling to realize I brought all
these talented people together.

Creating the music is just the beginning. Then comes publishing
rights, videos, streaming services, remixes, distribution, social media,
and on and on. There are so many angles about being on the business

side of things that I've had to learn quickly. Creativity comes naturally for me; the rest has been a learning process.

My friends always ask how I manage it all and how I handle the pressure. They'll say, "You've got your music company, you're touring with Kool & the Gang, and you're working on your solo stuff." It does sound like a lot that way, but when it's a labor of love, it brings me joy and fulfillment when others are a success. I want to see my artists succeed, and I know that with guidance, they will. That's where I'm coming from. It's all about the music, and it's from the heart.

We were in England when Marvin Gaye came onstage and sang with us. It was an amazing performance, and afterward, he came over to me and said, "Man, you can play some drums!" He knew what he was talking about, because he was a drummer himself, so he understood what goes into it. He was a few years older than me, and I respected him so much. His voice was so amazing. We smoked some herb together, and I told him, "Thank you for saying that. You're my idol and your support means so much to me."

The main reason I like to push myself creatively and work to mentor others is that I owe it to the craft and my gift. I try to honor it every day. I start each morning with a prayer of blessings to all beings to help me walk a better path and to be a better person. That's been my guiding light for all these years. It's allowed me to stay focused and present.

That spirituality fuels me and my music. I see myself as a Rosicrucian Kabbalist, and I belong to secret societies. I've been initiated into the science of spirituality. These are the things I vibe for. I meditate, and I pray for all. I feel it is important to pray for all humanity and all creation.

I am also asked to create music for films, either songs for the soundtrack or some or all of the score that is used throughout the movie. Sometimes it's a collaboration with other artists; other times it's a solo project. Either way, I love the chance to compose different types of music and work on various projects. It's a way to exercise the music muscle by challenging myself to create appropriate music with my flavor.

My solo project is completely different from anything I've done with Kool & the Gang. I've gotten positive responses from industry insiders who have heard it, so I'm excited to continue putting out fun, new music. I played the song "What If," which I wrote for my partner, Claude, who has worked with a ton of celebrated artists. He's the music guy. After he heard the song, the man broke down and cried in the studio. I was taken aback. "Oh, man," I said, "what's wrong? What's wrong?" He said, "That's a beautiful piece, Brother George."

The album is an idea, a concept. It combines up-tempo and mid-tempo songs. It's got a real vibe, and it feels good to showcase my voice to such positive responses. I went for a harsh, bluesy tone. Writing the songs was deeply personal, and it reminded me of what my mother used to say when she read my poems: "Oh, they're so sad."

"Well, Mother, we live in the ghetto. Did you think it was going to be like a Norman Rockwell thing? The dog, the decorations, Dad coming home with a Christmas tree?"

We all write what we know, and that's the only way to give a song heart and soul. I'm innately spiritual in all the things I say and do. Sometimes, the universe will do that to you, to every single one of us on this planet. It will set a fire under you to get you going, because otherwise, most of us won't do what we need to do. Sometimes, the universe has a way of showing us how to use our blessings. As far as I'm concerned, going after your dreams is always worth it.

For as long as I can remember, the blessing for me has been the gift of music. I don't necessarily like the label of "a creative," because I think that's just part of who I am. It's not a role I play or a job I fulfill. It started way back when I was just a kid seeing those musical notes dancing in my dreams. I've found that when I trust my instincts and let the feeling guide me, I stay true to myself, and my dreams come alive. Someone who isn't familiar with my work might just see an easygoing, six-foot-two Black guy, but the secret is to look beyond the physical. We all have so much going on that others do not understand.

Success, or being in the presence of success, does strange things to people. I'm a private person. I love to be with people and I love to talk, but I'm also reserved. In those moments, when I'm private, that's when I write and get things done. I become introspective, and I dig deep for inspiration. That's part of the work that goes into the job. Folks just see the success and don't understand all that goes into it, the years of hard work and practice, the decades of experience.

That initial success and stardom are amazing, but it eventually wears off. Like a sailor, you soon grow your sea legs and learn how to handle the unpredictable waves that crash against the side of the boat. It's your new reality. As time goes on, you settle into it. You have nerves, but those are the nerves to perform. At the same time, you're censoring yourself and enjoying it and making sure that the audience is with you and they're enjoying it.

Then you start getting recognized. "Hey, that chocolate guy is in the band." When they understand what I've accomplished, the whole dynamic changes. They become like purring cats that keep rubbing up against my leg.

Now I'm able to pour all that experience into my music. Putting my album together was the result of lots of prayer and blessings. It encompasses me as an artist and as a person. That comes out in the lyrics. One of the songs says, "What if you find that heaven's gates were closed forever and all the good you've done, no gain? Would you still strive to make this world a better place, or would you just shake the finger of blame in someone's face?"

When I was working on the album, I went full-bore into writing mode. Once I was happy with the songs, I moved to arranging, producing, and playing the instruments. I assembled the pieces of the puzzle, the puzzle of my collective experiences, my heritage, my life. It was a long, arduous, but ultimately satisfying experience. It feels amazing to create something so personal, and I hope it will resonate with others. I hope the music touches people and makes them feel something special. It's different from anything I've worked on. The dynamics are different, the collaborations are new, and the songs are more intimate, because I've put my heart and soul into each one.

I used the creative process as an opportunity to lose myself, to immerse myself in the music, and it brought up so many thoughts and memories. What does it mean to "lose yourself"? Does it happen when you "become" your profession? Or is it when you go out on your own and move to a new city, ready for your own adventures?

As a proud African American, I followed my own path. First I married within my race, but then I listened to my heart, marrying a Japanese woman, and now I have a Vietnamese wife. Stepping away from my race and culture initially felt like a betrayal, but I quickly realized that it was just the opposite. I was honoring my heritage and sharing my culture with others who shared theirs with me in turn. But I never forgot my beginnings, my roots.

When the freed slaves migrated north to New Jersey, New York, and the New England states, they primarily came from Virginia, North and South Carolina, and Georgia. Many former slaves from Alabama, Mississippi, and Louisiana went to Chicago, Arkansas, and Texas, while those from western Louisiana migrated to California and the Northwest. They shed the mind-set of slavery by seeking—and finding—a better life for their children, but they never forgot their past. How could they? But they had to evolve to survive.

Where we are raised also has an impact on how we perceive music. Those who settled in the Northeast brought with them traditional African melodies fused with English, Irish, and Scottish music. Those who landed in the Midwest were influenced by French, Spanish, and Portuguese mixed with gospel and delta blues. The generations that followed took that music and pioneered early genres like big band, swing, and jazz to today's music—rock, R&B, funk, dance, pop, rap, and hip-hop.

Would we have such musical variety without those former slaves bravely charting unfamiliar territory with little more than the clothes on their backs and the songs in their hearts? There's no doubt they changed and influenced the musical landscape of this country. Historically, Black people have done the same throughout the world with calypso, reggae, mambo, salsa, conga, bossa nova, and so on.

Those musical styles emerged from disenfranchised people, former African slaves, who fought to overcome the attempts to erase their rich, complex cultures as they realized that even their surnames had been changed to Brown, Williams, Johnson, Jackson, and Smith to erase their ancestral lineage. Despite those efforts, or possibly because of them, Black people became a greater part of the cultural landscape than their detractors could have ever predicted.

That magical, musical legacy certainly resonated with the six of us as eager young musicians with nothing to lose and everything to gain. We were set up for success by our ancestors, who settled in a new part of the country with only their stories and music to preserve such rich history. Armed with a similar sense of hope and determination, Kool & the Gang set out to make music that excited us and would, in turn, entertain and inspire others.

Fueled by the sheer tenacity of a group of Black teens from Jersey City, Kool & the Gang went on to make an indelible impact on popular music that has influenced several generations. The accolades are irrefutable—a star on the Hollywood Walk of Fame, induction in the Songwriters Hall of Fame, two Grammy Awards, and seven American Music Awards. That was the result of decades of hard work that ultimately yielded more than thirty albums that went gold and platinum, with twenty-five R&B hits and nine pop hits—so far.

It's not just that Kool & the Gang's music was a hit. Those songs have a rare staying power, because they have become part of our culture. Anthems like "Celebration," "Ladies' Night," "Fresh," and "Too Hot" are played at countless weddings, sporting events, and other celebrations where people want to have a good time.

After our 2015 induction into the New Jersey Hall of Fame at the Asbury Park Convention Hall, we went to the Watermark restaurant to relax with family and friends. While there, a young man walked over to congratulate us and said, "Now that you're at the finish line, what's next for you?"

I told him, "There is no finish line. Whatever field you have chosen has many routes, from the main road to the scenic highways. They all don't have to go in the same direction. It's better if they don't. How else would we experience all that life has to offer?"

On April 29, 2016, in our hometown of Jersey City, a street was named after our band. Kool & the Gang Way is located downtown, just off Pacific Avenue. Though we should all travel our own route and make our own way through this blessed life we are privileged to live, if you're in Jersey City and find yourself driving down Kool & the Gang Way, think of the six tenacious teenagers who banded together to conquer the world of music.

Thank you, heavenly father.

EPILOGUE

S URVIVING A HEALTH ISSUE is not only a glorious miracle but also a learning opportunity. When you tell people about it, the ones invested in your well-being will likely promise to pray for you. I've found that how people react to such devastating news can truly separate the wheat from the chaff. You learn rather quickly who truly cares and, unfortunately, who does not. It can be a sobering experience on top of medical worries. There's no question that the situation messes with your head in many ways.

Before cancer, I had to deal with the infection I discovered when I was driving home from the doctor. I was feeling much better until I began to feel chills pulsing through my body, and I could hardly focus. Fortunately, I made it to the driveway and put the car in park before I slumped over. My son saw me and called 911. I was shaking uncontrollably. My temperature was 103.5 degrees, and I was delirious.

Only a few months later, I was going through cancer, and that made me reflect on my past and, more important, my future. It gave me pause and allowed me to take stock of what's important and where my passions lie. Writing hit songs with the band has been so satisfying, and fortunately, I still find joy in that. I have heard from a lot of entertainers that their joy comes from their performances, their time onstage, but their personal lives are void of similar joy. Their only focus is to work until their next performance, where they will once again feel shiny and new.

I've learned that the awards can't keep you company. It's like a relationship where you both must put in the work to keep it together. Every time I was in a relationship, I never acted like a player, but many women I was with participated in nefarious nocturnal misadventures. They often confessed their clandestine relationships much later, after we had parted ways, a futile attempt to clear their consciences, I suppose. However, I knew that it wasn't me they had to make amends with, but themselves. They needed to examine how they moved through life and decide if it was working for them.

Growing up, I had a lot of obstacles standing in the way of my dream of being a successful musician. There was an alcoholic father, a family that didn't have much money, and no connections in the entertainment industry. Through hard work and perseverance, I was able to realize my dreams, but at what cost? I've traveled extensively for more than fifty years, and during that time I've missed graduations, birthdays, parties, and life's precious moments. It might seem glamorous at first, but travel gets the best of you. It always wins. When you're young, it's exciting, exhilarating even, but later it wears your ass out. The shows are glorious and the performances are fulfilling, but if that's all you have, you can end up feeling empty most of the time.

As I navigated my recent health scare, my wife was by my side, and as a medical professional, she was a pro at handling my appointments, collecting information from the doctors, and navigating the hospital red tape—not an easy feat. The people who came to see me were surprised by my rapid recovery. "You look great," one friend said. "I thought you would be bent over. You look the same."

I know people don't mean anything by comments like that. If they've never experienced the horrors of cancer, they don't know what to expect. My doctors attributed my progress to a life relatively free of vices. My last alcoholic drink was probably thirty-eight years ago. Same with cigarettes. I like to think my vegan lifestyle also contributed to my recovery. Being on the road can wreck your body, but I focus on working out, building strength, and improving flexibility.

Mentally, I've put in the work to stay focused and present. I get down at times, even now, but those episodes usually pass quickly. Going through cancer treatment can mess with your mind, and it's easy to succumb to the negativity. I've been in therapy for a long time, and it helps me cope with the hard times so I can enjoy the good times.

When I was laid up to rebuild my strength, I watched old shows like *Perry Mason* and *Gunsmoke* as a distraction. I like the way Perry Mason always solved a case or Matt Dillon was able to run the bad guys out of town. Those comfort shows reminded me of my mother and grandmother and the shows they watched on those bulky, wood-paneled, black-and-white console TVs. Working in my home studio also helped me recover by keeping my mind busy. My wife kept at me to rest more, but I just couldn't. That has never been one of my talents, even as a kid. My mind has always been too active for me to ignore.

I was ecstatic to learn after my surgery that the cancer had not spread to my lymph nodes. There was one tiny lesion that they removed before it metastasized. A few weeks of radiation and chemo followed as a preventative measure. It was a big surgery. They had to remove a lobe of my lung. The operation was performed through the miracle of robotics, as the mechanical arm navigated between my ribs to pierce my lung and remove the unwelcome trespasser. I'm grateful that it hadn't spread and that the follow-up treatments were relatively mild. The prognosis is that I'll have full capacity as the lung grows and learns to compensate for the portion that was removed.

After the procedure, I had painkillers to ease the discomfort as a tube drained the remaining fluid, which took several days. The biggest benefit of these advances in medicine is that I only had to stay in the hospital one night. Of course, the recovery was longer, but I was able to go to the dedicated VIP floor of a nearby rehab facility staffed with twenty-four-hour medical professionals.

It took some time to get used to my reduced breathing capacity. I took many tests to measure my lung function. My breathing has continued to improve, something I was initially concerned about as a performer. When I first came out of surgery, I was surprised to find that I had the faint breath of an infant, quick and shallow, but that gradually improved with practice and patience.

There was a machine that measured the strength of my lungs, and the goal was to reach five hundred on the breathing machine before I could move around. I used that machine once an hour until I hit my goal and earned my freedom. I was allowed to move around and get some exercise, so I got a ride to Neiman Marcus because I knew that would require lots of walking. I had to go much slower than I was used to, but I kept reminding myself to take it easy. I was alarmed at first when I couldn't catch my breath, but with a little patience, I got into an even rhythm of walking and breathing. It's not a sprint, it's a marathon.

After my excursion, I returned to the facility and realized I was quite a sight—a tall, dark-skinned man wearing sweats, with kinky hair, looking scruffy in the posh facility with Rolls-Royces and Bentleys parked out front.

"Where have you been?" the nurse asked. "We were concerned."

"Just getting a little exercise. I had to take my lungs for a test drive." I unpacked, downed my medicine like a good patient, and ordered a healthy dinner. The next day, my brother came by, and we went out. I followed a similar pattern for five days. Once they helped me out of bed, I was good to go. There was no stopping me at that point. I was determined to get some exercise, work on my breathing, and regain my strength.

I finally got to where I could get out of bed on my own. I just had to be careful to avoid the shooting pain I'd get if I put pressure on the wrong area of my body. The pain soon ebbed to little more than a twinge as I continued my rehabilitation, facilitated by some healthy foods and CBD oils. (I stayed away from edibles!)

When I was somewhat incapacitated, my true concern was for my family. I wanted to make sure that if anything happened, everything was in place so that my wife and my sons would be in a good spot. During this process, I realized that I wasn't scared of death but more of how it would affect those around me.

They went through a lot, because in five months I overcame several medical issues: kidney stones, stents, a biopsy, and the threat of tuberculosis. The mental toll that takes on not only the patient but the family and loved ones is not something one can prepare for, and everyone experiences it differently.

I knew that my recovery wasn't just physical but mental as well, for me and my family. When death looms, it can mess with your mind, and not everyone is equipped to cope with the repercussions, even if things turn out for the best. The emotional damage can linger, whether or not we choose to admit it.

During my illness and recovery, another change had been taking place. It's one meant to improve life, but it can also tear it apart. We were going through months of a house renovation that seemed to start small but grew quickly. If you've never had to experience the trials and tribulations of a renovation, consider yourself lucky.

My wife had waited for quite some time to make changes. I was fine with things the way they were, but life is about compromise. So while I dealt with health issues, those issues were compounded by the endless pounding of hammers and whirring of saws. Upgrading the house sounds good in theory, but the slow, extended torture can test anyone's mental resolve.

All I've been through lately made me realize that I know nothing, but I've accomplished so much. I know a lot but don't know anything. It's an Eastern philosophy that says the more you think you know, the less you really know.

I sometimes feel like the outlier in our family compound. My wife and sons know things because they have degrees. I have a degree in life. I come from the streets, where no matter how clean you are, your surroundings are still filthy.

I look at my kids and know they don't understand what that struggle was like. Here they are in a beautiful Los Angeles family compound with singers, ballplayers, and actors as neighbors. I've been able to provide a good education for each of them. My youngest wanted to play basketball, so I arranged for him to be trained by one of the Lakers.

Not long after I returned home, my oldest son and his mom fought, and he stayed out all night. I was worried and couldn't sleep, because parenting never ends, no matter how old they get. My brother said, "At first, I didn't understand why you went to the recovery place, and now I do. Peace of mind."

Before I was cleared to drive, I had a caretaker and driver from Zambia. Having a driver was supposed to help me get better by not having to worry about how to get around, but my man from Africa was not the best driver. I'd have to say things like "You're in the middle of the road" or "You just went through a stop sign."

I tried to make him comfortable by taking him out to eat so he could hopefully relax and maybe start following the traffic rules. We went to a popular breakfast spot called Leo & Lily, and he didn't understand the concept of valet parking. "Pull in here," I said. He kept swerving, and it wasn't helping my recovery. When it was time to order, I asked what he would like. "Anything," he responded. The waiter tried his luck, and my driver finally said, "You have meat and rice? Or soup?"

"What kind?" the patient man asked.

"Any kind."

I was told that all cancer patients are encouraged to speak to a therapist or psychologist to deal with the syndrome, similar to post-traumatic stress disorder, or PTSD, that can occur after such a traumatic experience. Another reason is that the medications, such as OxyContin and gamma-aminobutyric acid (GABA), help with recovery but have side effects that can include upset stomach, headache, sleepiness, muscle weakness, and physical addiction. They can also mess with your mind and alter your thoughts. It's important to wean oneself off them quickly. I was particularly focused on that because of the addiction I overcame years ago.

The main reason I've been so open about the cancer is that I realized I was blessed, and I'm thankful to the Creator. I feel it's my responsibility to use my platform to help others by sharing information. I think with success, it's incumbent upon people to help others any way they can, whether on a large or small scale. I hope to spread awareness.

Part of my recovery is knowing that I not only have an album coming out but also will be back on the road with my bandmates in Kool & the Gang. A psychologist once told me that you have to be out of your mind, in a good way, to be an artist. From the early days to now, more than five decades later, we still see the elation in each other's eyes as we play. Along with that comes an undercurrent of honest fear and an exhilarating ache that comes from taking the risk of expressing your art and having people understand you.

On most nights, when the band is cooking, I sit at the piano to the right of Kool and look over at him as he looks at me. We give each other the wink, our kind of thumbs up. It's a connection that goes way back to the beginning. It feels as valuable as any grand reward.

Without that, we would never have sold seventy million records worldwide, won Grammys, and achieved the fame associated with creating music that people have loved for generations.

That connection is more important today, because Kool and I are the two surviving original members of the band. The painful part of being in a group for so long is that we've lost several key members who were so much more than bandmates—they were true brothers. Dennis passed in August 2021, Ronald (Khalis) Bell died in September 2020, and we also lost Ricky Westfield and Charles "Claydes" Smith. Other important members have passed as well, but we've been fortunate to find talented musicians who preserve the spirit of the band as we pay tribute to the members who have crossed over every time we play.

I believe that nothing happens by mistake. Sometimes, we need a little convincing to accept the fact that we are together for a reason. Call it divine intervention if you wish, because that is how it feels. Like any relationship, and especially those that span several decades, problems big and small have come up, and it hasn't always been smooth, but the spirituality we share in the act of writing and playing together ultimately outweighs any issues.

Looking back from those earliest moments to the present, I can marvel at how things came together in ways that seem nothing short of miraculous. Life can feel like an exercise in randomness, but what unfolds hardly feels accidental. No doubt our sense of purpose, our passion, and our hard work kept us on a clear path and created their own momentum. One thing led to another. Even experiences of devastating adversity have hidden blessings. Special people came into our lives to help at just the right time. Now, decades later, we are in many ways no different than the teenagers we were when we first met. We still carry within us that same curiosity, excitement, and wonderment, and most important, we strive to learn and improve.

Another important thing I took away from therapy is to embrace my individuality, which is not something we typically learn growing up. We strive so hard to fit in, but I was also seen as "different." Classmates said it, women I dated said it, and even band management said it. That label has followed me throughout my life, and I never completely understood it.

How am I different? Maybe it began when I was put in high school with a predominantly Caucasian student body. There were only four Black kids, and we banded together immediately. Given that the school was in a different part of the city, the curriculum was different from the inner-city schools. We learned Latin and even sang Christmas songs like "O Come, All Ye Faithful" in Latin. Who does that? My neighborhood friends certainly didn't.

The more I heard that I was different, the closer I came to accepting it. Then in therapy I learned that historically, creative people have been viewed as different because of their expression of talent. The ability to see the world with a new perspective can be threatening to some folks. Understanding that helped me to better deal with those comments.

After traveling all over the world and playing for all types of audiences, I've learned that the true portrait of America is one of diversity and inclusion. We're a melting pot of all races and religions. That's who we are. We're all in this together. That's what keeps this country great, and I love looking out from the stage and seeing every hue of skin represented in those eager, appreciative, devoted audiences. It's one big, beautiful, multicultural celebration of love.

Here we are, a group of Black men who have worked hard to create a music powerhouse that has lasted for decades and entertained generations of music lovers. The power of music surprises me at every concert, the way it can bring people together and show them how much they have in common, instead of the differences that drive them apart.

After every show, I just hope the people in the audience take that unity and goodwill with them and apply it to their everyday lives.

DISCOGRAPHY

George Brown

What If
"We Don't Need a Reason"
"What If"
"Your Body"
"Hands Up"
"My Woman"
"Honey"
"She Just Wants"
"Leave It on the Fire"
"Gemma"
"Everything You Do"

Kool & the Gang

1969

Kool & the Gang
"Kool & the Gang"

"The Gang's Back Again"
"Kool's Back Again"

1971

Live at the Sex Machine
"Let the Music Take Your Mind"
"Funky Man"
"Who's Gonna Take the Weight"
"I Want to Take You Higher"

Live at PJ's
"N.T. Part I"

1972

Music Is the Message
"Love the Life You Live, Part 1"
"Music Is the Message, Part 1"
"Funky Granny"

Good Times
"Good Times"

1973

Wild and Peaceful
"Funky Stuff"
"Jungle Boogie"
"Hollywood Swinging"

1974

Light of Worlds
"Summer Madness"
"Winter Sadness"

1975

Spirit of the Boogie
"Spirit of the Boogie"
"Caribbean Festival"

1976

Love and Understanding
"Hollywood Swinging (live)"
"Summer Madness (live)"
"Universal Sound (live)"

Open Sesame
"Open Sesame"
"Super Band"

1977

The Force
"The Force"

1978

Everybody's Dancin'
"Everybody's Dancin'"

1979

Ladies' Night
"Ladies' Night"
"Too Hot"

1980

Celebrate!
"Celebration"

1981

Something Special
"Take My Heart"
"Get Down on It"
"Steppin' Out"
"Stand Up and Sing"

1982

As One
"Let's Go Dancin'"
"Big Fun"

1983

In the Heart
"Joanna"
"Straight Ahead"
"Tonight"

1984

Emergency
"Fresh"
"Misled"
"Emergency"
"Cherish"

1986

Forever
"Victory"
"Stone Love"
"Holiday"
"Special Way"
"Peacemaker"

1989

Sweat
"Raindrops"
"Never Give Up"

1993

Unite
"(Jump Up on the) Rhythm
and Ride"

1996

State of Affairs
"Salute to the Ladies"

2001

Gangland
"Big Thangs"

2007

Still Kool
"Dave"
"Steppin' into Love"

INDEX